Measuring Efficiency: An Assessment of Data Envelopment Analysis

Richard H. Silkman, *Editor*
University of Southern Maine

NEW DIRECTIONS FOR PROGRAM EVALUATION
A Publication of the American Evaluation Association
A joint organization of the Evaluation Research Society and the Evaluation Network
MARK W. LIPSEY, *Editor-in-Chief*
Claremont Graduate School

Number 32, Winter 1986

Paperback sourcebooks in
The Jossey-Bass Higher Education and
Social and Behavioral Sciences Series

Ministry of Education, Ontario
Information Centre, 13th Floor,
Mowat Block, Queen's Park,
Toronto, Ont.   M7A 1L2

Jossey-Bass Inc., Publishers
San Francisco • London

Richard H. Silkman (ed.).
Measuring Efficiency: An Assessment of Data Envelopment Analysis.
New Directions for Program Evaluation, no. 32.
San Francisco: Jossey-Bass, 1986.

New Directions for Program Evaluation Series
A publication of the American Evaluation Association
Mark W. Lipsey, *Editor-in-Chief*

Copyright © 1986 by Jossey-Bass Inc., Publishers
and
Jossey-Bass Limited

Copyright under International, Pan American, and Universal
Copyright Conventions. All rights reserved. No part of
this issue may be reproduced in any form—except for brief
quotation (not to exceed 500 words) in a review or professional
work—without permission in writing from the publishers.

New Directions for Program Evaluation (publication number USPS
449-050) is published quarterly by Jossey-Bass Inc., Publishers, and is
sponsored by the American Evaluation Association. Second-class
postage rates are paid at San Francisco, California, and at
additional mailing offices. POSTMASTER: Send address changes
to Jossey-Bass Inc., Publishers, 433 California Street, San Francisco,
California 94104.

Editorial correspondence should be sent to the Editor-in-Chief,
Mark Lipsey, Psychology Department, Claremont Graduate School,
Claremont, Calif. 91711.

Library of Congress Catalog Card Number LC 85-81900

International Standard Serial Number ISSN 0164-7989

International Standard Book Number ISBN 1-55542-991-2

Cover art by WILLI BAUM

Manufactured in the United States of America

Ordering Information

The paperback sourcebooks listed below are published quarterly and can be ordered either by subscription or single copy.

Subscriptions cost $40.00 per year for institutions, agencies, and libraries. Individuals can subscribe at the special rate of $30.00 per year *if payment is by personal check*. (Note that the full rate of $40.00 applies if payment is by institutional check, even if the subscription is designated for an individual.) Standing orders are accepted.

Single copies are available at $9.95 when payment accompanies order. (California, New Jersey, New York, and Washington, D.C., residents please include appropriate sales tax.) For billed orders, cost per copy is $9.95 plus postage and handling.

Substantial discounts are offered to organizations and individuals wishing to purchase bulk quantities of Jossey-Bass sourcebooks. Please inquire.

Please note that these prices are for the academic year 1986-1987 and are subject to change without prior notice. Also, some titles may be out of print and therefore not available for sale.

To ensure correct and prompt delivery, all orders must give either the *name of an individual* or an *official purchase order number*. Please submit your order as follows:

Subscriptions: specify series and year subscription is to begin.
Single Copies: specify sourcebook code (such as, PE1) and first two words of title.

Mail orders for United States and Possessions, Latin America, Canada, Japan, Australia, and New Zealand to:
Jossey-Bass Inc., Publishers
433 California Street
San Francisco, California 94104

Mail orders for all other parts of the world to:
Jossey-Bass Limited
28 Banner Street
London EC1Y 8QE

New Directions for Program Evaluation
Mark W. Lipsey, *Editor-in-Chief*

PE1 *Exploring Purposes and Dimensions,* Scarvia B. Anderson, Claire D. Coles
PE2 *Evaluating Federally Sponsored Programs,* Charlotte C. Rentz, R. Robert Rentz
PE3 *Monitoring Ongoing Programs,* Donald L. Grant

PE4 *Secondary Analysis,* Robert F. Boruch
PE5 *Utilization of Evaluative Information,* Larry A. Braskamp, Robert D. Brown
PE6 *Measuring the Hard-to-Measure,* Edward H. Loveland
PE7 *Values, Ethics, and Standards in Evaluation,* Robert Perloff, Evelyn Perloff
PE8 *Training Program Evaluators,* Lee Sechrest
PE9 *Assessing and Interpreting Outcomes,* Samuel Ball
PE10 *Evaluation of Complex Systems,* Ronald J. Wooldridge
PE11 *Measuring Effectiveness,* Dan Baugher
PE12 *Federal Efforts to Develop New Evaluation Methods,* Nick L. Smith
PE13 *Field Assessments of Innovative Evaluation Methods,* Nick L. Smith
PE14 *Making Evaluation Research Useful to Congress,* Leonard Saxe, Daniel Koretz
PE15 *Standards for Evaluation Practice,* Peter H. Rossi
PE16 *Applications of Time Series Analysis to Evaluation,* Garlie A. Forehand
PE17 *Stakeholder-Based Evaluation,* Anthony S. Bryk
PE18 *Management and Organization of Program Evaluation,* Robert G. St. Pierre
PE19 *Philosophy of Evaluation,* Ernest R. House
PE20 *Developing Effective Internal Evaluation,* Arnold J. Love
PE21 *Making Effective Use of Mailed Questionnaires,* Daniel C. Lockhart
PE22 *Secondary Analysis of Available Data Bases,* David J. Bowering
PE23 *Evaluating the New Information Technologies,* Jerome Johnston
PE24 *Issues in Data Synthesis,* William H. Yeaton, Paul M. Wortman
PE25 *Culture and Evaluation,* Michael Quinn Patton
PE26 *Economic Evaluations of Public Programs,* James S. Catterall
PE27 *Utilizing Prior Research in Evaluation Planning,* David S. Cordray
PE28 *Randomization and Field Experimentation,* Robert F. Boruch, Werner Wothke
PE29 *Teaching Evaluation Across the Disciplines,* Barbara Gross Davis
PE30 *Naturalistic Evaluation,* David D. Williams
PE31 *Advances in Quasi-Experimental Design and Analysis,* William M. K. Trochim

Contents

Editor's Notes 1
Richard H. Silkman

1. The Methodology of Data Envelopment Analysis 7
Thomas R. Sexton

This chapter provides both a graphical and an analytical introduction to data envelopment analysis (DEA). The basic concepts and key issues are illustrated with a simple hypothetical example using nursing homes.

2. Managing Productivity of Health Care Organizations 31
H. David Sherman

This chapter illustrates the usefulness of data envelopment analysis as a management tool in the health care sector.

3. An Exploratory Analysis of Variations in Performance Among 47
U.S. National Parks
Eduardo L. Rhodes

This chapter demonstrates how data envelopment analysis can be used to evaluate the performance efficiencies of public parks.

4. Data Envelopment Analysis: Critique and Extensions 73
Thomas R. Sexton, Richard H. Silkman, Andrew J. Hogan

This chapter discusses some of the shortcomings and problem areas of data envelopment analysis and provides a variety of methodological enhancements that can improve the application of DEA.

Index 107

New Directions for Program Evaluation

A Quarterly Publication of the American Evaluation Association
(A Joint Organization of the Evaluation Research Society and
the Evaluation Network)

Editor-in-Chief:

Mark W. Lipsey, Psychology, Claremont Graduate School

Editorial Advisory Board:

Scarvia B. Andersen, Psychology, Georgia Institute of Technology
Gerald L. Barkdoll, U.S. Food and Drug Administration, Washington D.C.
Robert F. Boruch, Psychology, Northwestern University
Timothy C. Brock, Psychology, Ohio State University
Donald T. Campbell, Social Relations, Lehigh University
Eleanor Chelimsky, U.S. General Accounting Office, Washington D.C.
James A. Ciarlo, Mental Health Systems Evaluation, University of Denver
Ross F. Conner, Social Ecology, University of California, Irvine
William W. Cooley, Learning Research and Development Center, University of Pittsburgh
David S. Cordray, Psychology, Northwestern University
Robert W. Covert, Evaluation Research Center, University of Virginia
Lois-ellin Datta, U.S. General Accounting Office, Washington D.C.
Barbara Gross Davis, Educational Development, University of California, Berkeley
Howard E. Freeman, Sociology, University of California, Los Angeles
Egon G. Guba, Education, Indiana University
Edward S. Halpern, AT&T Bell Laboratories, Naperville, Illinois
Harry P. Hatry, The Urban Institute, Washington D.C.
Michael Hendricks, MH Associates, Washington D.C.
Gary T. Henry, Joint Legislative Audit and Review Commission, Virginia
Dennis H. Holmes, Education, George Washington University
Ernest R. House, CIRCE, University of Illinois, Urbana-Champaign
Jeanette M. Jerrell, Cognos Associates, Los Altos, California
Karen E. Kirkhart, Educational Psychology, University of Texas, Austin
Henry M. Levin, Education, Stanford University
Richard J. Light, Government, Harvard University
Charles McClintock, Human Service Studies, Cornell University
William A. McConnell, San Francisco Community Mental Health Programs
Jeri Nowakowski, Leadership and Education Policy Studies, Northern Illinois University
Michael Q. Patton, International Programs, University of Minnesota

Charles S. Reichardt, Psychology, University of Denver
Leonard Rutman, Price Waterhouse Associates, Ottawa, Ontario
Thomas A. Schwandt, Arthur Andersen & Co., St. Charles, Illinois
Penny Sebring, NORC, University of Chicago
Lee Sechrest, Psychology, University of Arizona
Jana Kay Smith, Affordable Health Care Concepts, Sacramento, California
Midge F. Smith, Agricultural and Extension Education, University of Maryland
Nick L. Smith, Education, Syracuse University
Robert E. Stake, CIRCE, University of Illinois, Urbana-Champaign
Robert M. Stonehill, U.S. Department of Education
Daniel L. Stufflebeam, Evaluation Center, Western Michigan University
Robert St. Pierre, Abt Associates, Inc., Cambridge, Massachusetts
Carol H. Weiss, Education, Harvard University
Joseph S. Wholey, School of Public Administration, University of Southern California
Paul M. Wortman, ISR/CRUSK, University of Michigan
William H. Yeaton, ISR/CRUSK, University of Michigan

American Evaluation Association, 9555 Persimmon Tree Road, Potomac, MD 20854

Editor's Notes

If eras can be neatly labeled, then the present era (by which I mean the last decade or so) must be called the Era of Efficiency. And, if each era can be said to have a manifesto, then a leading contender for that role in the present era is certainly *War on Waste: President's Private Sector Survey on Cost Control* (1984), which is more commonly referred to as the Grace Commission. Indeed, the report itself reads like a manifesto: It details deplorable conditions, identifies villains and perpetrators, lays out an agenda for change, and offers the promise of better tomorrows. But, what is most striking about the report and the activities of the commission that produced it is the ability to identify and quantify waste and inefficiency in our government. The commission has done what few academics have been able to do, especially on such a large scale: It has separated inefficiency from quality and undesired quality from desired quality—and without the benefit of a single demand curve. Its conclusion is that one-third of all federal taxes is consumed by waste and inefficiency in the federal government.

Clearly, this is a very serious indictment of our federal government—its agencies, administrators, and employees. However, it is equally clear to those who have studied government operations that the identification and measurement of inefficiency in government is a difficult task that must be undertaken with only the greatest of caution and care. We recognize the very serious problems associated with estimating the efficiency with which organizations and agencies provide services in the public sector. These problems range from the conceptual (what is the appropriate measure of a government agency's output?; what do educational institutions or halfway houses produce?), to the practical (are there data that we can use to measure efficiency?; what longitudinal information do we have that will allow us to assess the consequences of different treatments?; what modeling or similation has been performed to determine the impact of closing branch offices?). The concerns include such issues as the measurement of quality gradations; the absence of market prices to compute, aggregate, and compare the economic values of outputs; and the recognition and inclusion of costs that are external (in addition to those that are internal) to the organization or agency. Thus, we approach a report such as that of the Grace Commission with substantial skepticism, not because we question the motives of the authors or the nature of their conclusions (although both deserve careful scrutiny) but rather because we know from personal experience that it is difficult for an outside observer to evaluate the efficiency and effectiveness of a single department, let alone an entire agency. Our collective experience has left us humbled but unbowed. We have learned a great deal from our efforts to evaluate the performance of government agencies. First and foremost, we have learned just how painfully difficult it is to measure inefficiency or ineffectiveness in the public and nonmarket sectors.

I think it is fair to say that our difficulty derives in large measure from the absence of both high-quality data and of analytically sound methodology. Indeed, the most troublesome issue is the kernel of the problem: It is difficult to distinguish between waste or inefficiency on the one hand and high quality on the other since each is often manifested as high total or per unit costs. In the final analysis, all our methodologies require the generally heroic assumption that the variables have been appropriately defined and accurately measured, that the statistical results have not been biased by omitted variables or spurious correlation, that the production process is well understood and that it has been well specified, that the goals and objectives of the organization or agency have been correctly and completely incorporated, and that all internal and external factors have been accounted for.

Just as we are skeptical of the Grace Commission report, we are skeptical of any new methodology for measuring the efficiency with which organizations or agencies provide public goods and services that does not explicitly set forth the same assumption requirements as our traditional methodologies. Our natural skepticism requires us to scrutinize the methodology closely. When that methodology moves from the laboratory to the field, where it is applied in a policy analytic context, the need for such inspection becomes urgent. Such is the case with data envelopment analysis (DEA), a linear programming technique recently advanced in the Operations research literature by Charnes, Cooper, and Rhodes (1978, 1981).

Data envelopment analysis is a mathematical technique based on the principles of linear programming theory and application that is designed to assess how efficiently a firm, organization, agency, program site, or other such decision-making unit produces the outputs that it has been charged to produce. In brief, each producing unit is compared with all other producing units in the sample. A producing unit is said to be efficient if the ratio of its weighted outputs to its weighted inputs is greater than or equal to a similar ratio of outputs to inputs for every other producing unit in the sample. That is, for a given set of input and output weights, no other producing unit can transform as little input into as much output. Of course, certain constraints are placed on the input and output weights. In particular, each producing unit is free to choose any set of weights that it wishes provided, first, that the weights are nonnegative (certain authors have argued that the weights must be strictly positive) and, second, that no producing unit can be more than 100 percent efficient (the choice of weights cannot result in that unit's or any other unit's ratio of weighted output to weighted input exceeding one). Thus, the objective for each producing unit is to choose the set of weights that maximizes its efficiency rating without making its own or any other unit's efficiency rating greater than one.

The reader will note that this new efficiency measure is both similar to and different from the more commonly applied ratio measure. Both measures are constructed in the same way, that is, as the ratio of weighted outputs to weighted inputs. They differ in the selection of weights. The traditional measure relies on values or market prices as weights. As a result, the ratio often becomes simply the total value of all outputs produced divided by the total value of all inputs used in their production. Further, under the traditional measure, the producing unit has no choice of input and output weights. Its weights are not applied to other producing units, and it is not subject to the weights of other producing units. In contrast, under DEA each producing unit selects its own weights, subject to the two conditions noted earlier. (This issue is explored in detail in Chapter Four.)

Data envelopment analysis uses the set of producing units in the sample to construct a production or efficiency frontier consisting of all possible linear combinations of efficient producing units. By definition, then, any point on the frontier represents a feasible technique for efficiently combining the set of inputs to produce a given set of outputs. Such a technique is feasible since it reflects only the practices of existing producing units, and it is efficient since it is defined exclusively in terms of the techniques used by efficient producing units. Producing units that are not on the frontier are said to be inefficient in direct proportion to their distance from the frontier. Thus, for a given set of weights, a producing unit that uses twice as much of each input to produce the same amount of outputs as an efficient unit is half as efficient and thus has an efficiency score of 0.5. (A simple diagrammatic exposition of this relationship is provided in Chapter One.) A similar efficiency score can be computed for each producing unit in the sample. Further, the DEA methodology provides very valuable managerial information that indicates how inefficient producing units can be made efficient through changes in resource deployment, output mix, or both.

The purpose of this *New Directions for Program Evaluation* sourcebook is to introduce data envelopment analysis to members of the evaluation community. My hope is that, by removing the technique from its origins and separating it from its creators and nursemaids, it will be more accessible, less intimidating, and better understood by what I believe to be its natural audience. This is not to suggest that DEA is best viewed absent its mathematical formulation and analytical rigor. In fact, I would argue that DEA can be used effectively only by those who are familiar with its structure, power, and limitations and that this familiarity can be achieved only by understanding its mathematical specification and operation. Yet, it is clear that, for many members of the evaluation community, the language and formulation of DEA, as they exist currently in the operations research literature, present serious impediments to adoption and use of the technique.

Accordingly, certain chapters in this volume, in particular Chapters One and Four, have a textbook flavor. While I recognize that this is unusual for publications in this series, I nevertheless feel that a textbook-like characterization of DEA is necessary. The reader will also note that the characterization of DEA proceeds at different levels of mathematical sophistication. The intent is to deliver the technique to the audience in a variety of packages so as to ensure the widest possible reception. Thus, in Chapter One, Thomas R. Sexton describes the most basic of DEA problems—a one-output, two-input formulation. This kind of problem readily lends itself to graphical exposition and solution. The uninitiated will need to follow the logic, the structure, and even the language of this most straightforward of DEA problems closely and carefully. Only after this initial graphical presentation is completed is the reader introduced to the more general mathematical formulation of the problem, which is illustrated by a more complicated but nevertheless straightforward two-output, two-input example. The final sections of Chapter One require readers to have a basic grounding in linear programming theory. An understanding of the relationship between what are called the *primal* and *dual* specifications of a linear programming problem is essential. The reader who does not possess such an understanding can skip this material without sacrificing a basic working understanding of DEA. However, in order both to make full use of the power of DEA and to avoid its many pitfalls and problems, the reader needs at least a basic familiarity with linear programming theory.

Chapter One provides a foundation for understanding the applications of DEA presented in Chapters Two and Three. In Chapter Two, H. David Sherman presents the results of an application of data envelopment analysis to the medical-surgical areas of a small sample of Massachusetts teaching hospitals. In Chapter Three, Eduardo L. Rhodes documents his application of DEA to a very broad sample of U.S. national parks. Both authors conclude that DEA is a very useful technique for gaining an understanding of productive and managerial efficiencies in public or nonmarket sectors of the economy. At the same time, both authors caution against indiscriminant use of the technique. They advise that it should be used in conjunction with other techniques, first, because DEA addresses only a limited set of issues relevant for any assessment of program or agency efficacy; second, because the technique is so powerful and subject to a wide array of specification-type problems.

Chapter Four begins where each of the first three chapters leaves off. First, Sexton, Silkman, and Hogan provide a general critique of data envelopment analysis. They point out two key issues: its exclusive concern with technical as opposed to price efficiency and its high degree of sensitivity to the most common forms of what can be called *specification error*. Then, the authors present a variety of extensions to the basic DEA framework. While certain of these extensions considerably increase the complexity of the technique, they serve as useful reminders of the shortcomings and limitations of DEA.

As I worked to assemble the contents of this volume, I was struck by the many similarities between data envelopment analysis today and regression analysis two decades ago. Twenty years ago, regression analysis promised to elevate substantially social science research, and in particular the art of evaluation. The technique offered the ability to analyze multiple, compound, and interactive relationships quantitatively. Over time, as user-friendly computer software helped to overcome the computational hurdles, increasing numbers of researchers and evaluators used the technique in a variety of situations and circumstances. This diffusion led in turn to modifications, extensions, and improvements on the basic regression framework. (The very term *ordinary least squares* highlights this phenomenon.) However, this diffusion also resulted in many misapplications of regression analysis, a problem that easy-to-use and essentially costless computer packages have exacerbated. I am certain that each of us can point to a number of examples in which regression analysis has been used or interpreted inappropriately.

Data envelopment analysis today resembles regression analysis twenty years ago. Its promise for solving many of the measurement problems that have plagued research on productivity measurement in the public and nonmarket sectors of the economy is especially important in view of our current overriding concern for efficiency in government. At present, use of DEA is being restrained by its mathematical complexity and by the absence of user-friendly computer software packages. Over the next five years, I would expect such software to be developed and to become more widespread. And, as we have seen with regression analysis, the diffusion of such software eliminates the mathematical complexity barriers as well (how many multiple regression users can demonstrate the "Best Linear Unbiased Estimator" (BLUE) property of OLS estimates not to mention the derivations of autocorrelation correction procedures, for example?) I would also expect that ten years from now each of us will be able to point to a number of examples in which data envelopment analysis has been used or interpreted inappropriately. My hope is that this volume will reduce the incidence of such inappropriate uses or interpretations even as it serves to stimulate the diffusion of data envelopment analysis.

Richard H. Silkman
Editor

References

Charnes, A., Cooper, W. W., and Rhodes, E. "Measuring the Efficiency of Decision-Making Units." *European Journal of Operations Research,* 1978, *2* (6), 429-444.

Charnes, A., Cooper, W. W., and Rhodes, E. "Evaluating Program and Managerial Efficiency: An Application of Data Envelopment Analysis to Program Follow Through." *Management Science,* 1981, *27* (6), 668-697.

Grace, P. J. *War on Waste: President's Private Sector Survey on Cost Control.* New York: Macmillan, 1984.

Richard H. Silkman is associate professor of public policy and management in the Graduate Program of Public Policy and Management at the University of Southern Maine, Portland.

Data envelopment analysis is a linear programming-based method that has clear advantages over competing approaches. However, its own limitations should not be overlooked.

The Methodology of Data Envelopment Analysis

Thomas R. Sexton

This chapter describes the methodology of data envelopment analysis (DEA) and shows how it relates to other procedures often used for the same purposes. I will indicate the ways in which DEA is superior to these other methods, and I will also point out its limitations. We will see that DEA is a linear programming–based methodology and hence that the necessary computations can be performed easily on any computer or microcomputer for which we have the appropriate software.

The problem at hand can be described as follows: An analyst wishes to measure the relative productive efficiency, or productivity, of each member of a set of comparable producing units, called *decision-making units* (DMUs). These decision-making units can be separate institutions or firms, such as police departments or hospitals, or they can be separate sites or branches of a single program or agency, such as classrooms or schools within a city school district or local Head Start programs. Each DMU uses a number of different inputs to produce a variety of different outputs, and there can be considerable flexibility in the manner in which individual DMUs combine inputs to produce outputs. In addition, natural costs and prices may be lacking for some or all the inputs and outputs, especially those which are not traded in markets. This is especially common in public and not-for-profit applications.

For example, a health systems analyst might be concerned with the relative efficiencies of a number of nursing homes in a certain state. Each nursing home is a DMU that combines several inputs (nursing hours at various skill levels, physician hours, supplies, and so forth) to produce several outputs (patient days disaggregated in some manner, such as diagnosis or method of payment). Even if unit costs and prices could be associated with each input and output (for example, wage rates for labor, unit costs for supplies, reimbursement rates for patient days), their usefulness in measuring efficiency would be questionable when the set of DMUs included not-for-profit and public as well as proprietary nursing homes. In other cases, such costs and prices may not even exist. For example, in education applications, the outputs could include average standardized test scores in a number of subjects, while the inputs could include measures of parental education or socioeconomic status. None of these outputs or inputs is directly priceable, since none is explicitly traded in a market. While each is scarce and hence of value to society, relative to one another and to other goods and services their values are unknown and arguably unknowable.

Present Methods for Measuring Efficiency

Two procedures other than data envelopment analysis are commonly used to measure efficiency: ratio analysis and multiple regression. Each suffers in important ways from a number of different problems that prohibit it from being used effectively in certain situations. DEA overcomes or alleviates many of these shortcomings while introducing a few new difficulties of its own.

Ratio Analysis. Historically, simple ratios have usually been used to perform efficiency measurement. For example, the health system analyst in the example just cited might compute the ratio between the total cost incurred by a nursing home in a given period of time to the number of patient days that the home has provided within the same period. But, this ratio is woefully inadequate when it is used to compare nursing homes. First, it fails to account for regional differences in the cost of living and in input markets, particularly the labor market. Obviously, costs per day are much higher in a nursing home in Manhattan than they are, say, in a small town in upstate New York. Second, this ratio treats all patient days as if they were identical. In fact, the severity of a patient's condition can greatly affect the resources required for treatment, and hence the cost of that treatment. The first shortcoming is often compensated for with varying degrees of success by cost of living and wage rate adjustments. The second shortcoming presents a much more serious problem.

To account for the multi-input, multi-output nature of such organizations as nursing homes, analysts usually compute several ratios simultaneously. For example, one could examine the hours of nursing labor used per patient day or the cost of supplies used per patient day. Individually, these ratios suffer from problems like those outlined earlier. Collectively, they tend to present a morass of numbers that give no clear indication of true efficiency. For example, if a particular nursing home owns the latest high-technology patient-monitoring system, the total cost per patient day may be high. But, as a result, it may also have a low ratio of nursing labor per patient day. One ratio suggests that the home is relatively less efficient; the other ratio makes the home seem relatively more efficient. Such ambiguity makes ratio analysis ineffective in efficiency evaluations.

Multiple Regression. As an alternative, analysts can use multiple regression analysis to model the output level of an organization or an agency (total patient days in the nursing home example) as a function of the various input levels. Such an analysis produces an estimated relationship that can be used to compute the predicted output level of a particular decision-making unit, given its input levels. DMUs that are relatively efficient lie above this relationship; that is, they produce more output than the model predicts, given their input levels. Conversely, relatively inefficient DMUs lie below the relationship, since they produce less output than their input levels lead us to predict. Relatively efficiency, therefore, is reflected in the residuals. Positive residuals indicate relative efficiency, while negative residuals indicate relative inefficiency.

There are three principal drawbacks to this approach. First, single-equation regression analysis requires that there be only one output or that all outputs be combined into a single indicator of production. In the nursing home example, this means that some sort of weighting scheme must be introduced to account for severity of illness or case mix. For example, does a nursing home that provides 100 days of skilled nursing care and 100 days of intermediate care produce more, less, or the same output as another nursing home that produces 50 and 150 days of care, respectively? Multiple-equation regression models can be used, but then there are multiple sets of residuals and no clear way of interpreting them in terms of efficiency. Second, regression analysis measures efficiency relative to average performance rather than best performance. Hence, it provides little direct information concerning the magnitudes of efficiency gains that are possible at various decision-making units within the sample. Finally, regression analysis requires the parametric specification of a production function, that is, an equation detailing how inputs are combined to produce outputs. In our example, the appropriate mathematical form for the nursing home industry production function is largely unknown. It is difficult to say on average, let alone at the margin, how nursing homes combine or could combine their inputs to produce outputs. Yet, the technique requires such a specification, which introduces an important source of error that can weaken the entire analysis. Consequently, multiple regression analysis is often inadequate for the analysis of efficiency.

Data Envelopment Analysis

Data envelopment analysis is a procedure that has been designed specifically to measure relative efficiency in situations in which there are multiple inputs and outputs and there is no obvious objective way of aggregating either inputs or outputs into a meaningful index of productive efficiency. The procedure has been applied in such diverse fields as education (Bessent and others, 1982), electricity production (Fare and Primont, 1984), criminal justice (Lewin and others, 1982), recreation (Rhodes, 1982), and health care (Sherman, 1984; Nunamaker, 1983). The technique is well documented in the management science literature (Charnes and others, 1978, 1979, 1981; Forsund and others, 1980), and it has received increasing attention as researchers have wrestled with problems of productivity measurement, especially in the services and nonmarket sectors of our economy.

In DEA, the relative efficiency of an organization, agency, or program site is defined as the ratio of its total weighted output to its total weighted input. The question is, How should one select the weights if no unit values can be assigned to the inputs or outputs? Herein lies the kernel of the DEA procedure. DEA permits each decision-making unit to select any weights that it wants for each input and output, provided that they satisfy certain reasonable conditions. These conditions are of two types: First, no weight can be negative. Second, the weights must be universal. Universality means that any DMU should be able to use the same set of weights to evaluate its own ratio or weighted output to weighted input and that the resulting ratio does not exceed one.

Each DMU, therefore, has considerable latitude in measuring its own efficiency; there are many sets of acceptable weights from which it can choose. In fact, each DMU chooses from exactly the same sets. DEA assumes that each DMU will select the weights that maximize its own efficiency score, that is, it will evaluate each input and each output in such a way as to maximize the ratio of its own weighted output to its own weighted input. Because different DMUs use different combinations of inputs to produce different combinations of outputs, we expect different DMUs to select sets of weights that reflect this variety. Generally, DMUs will place higher weights on the inputs that they use least and on the outputs that they produce most.

A word of caution is needed here concerning the interpretation of weights that a given DMU selects. These weights are not the values of inputs and outputs in any economic sense. Rather, they represent the weighting scheme that maximizes the efficiency of the DMU. If the DMUs were profit-maximizing firms and if each input and output had a unit cost and a unit sale price, then we might expect to find them using less of the costlier inputs and producing more of the higher-priced outputs, and this would follow the pattern expected in the weights. But we are dealing with DMUs operating under very different conditions, and such logical leaps are to be avoided.

The DEA model for a specific DMU can be formulated as a linear fractional program, which can easily be solved if it is transformed into an equivalent linear program in which the DMU's input and output weights are the decision variables. The simplex method is then used to solve the transformed linear program. A number of computer software packages are available for this purpose. Two packages are widely available for mainframe computer systems: the Functional Mathematical Programming System (FMPS) and the International Mathematical Subroutine Library (IMSL). DEA can also be run on a microcomputer by adapting microcomputer versions of these or other linear programming packages. Unfortunately, there is as yet no commercially available software that is specialized to run DEA-type analyses. In all cases, the user must adapt linear programming software packages to the specific requirements of data envelopment analysis. I have found that this is a straightforward exercise for someone who has a general understanding of computer systems and a working knowledge of such a language as FORTRAN. Users who lack such knowledge will require technical assistance in setting up the computer program routines in order to take full advantage of the power and capabilities of DEA.

A complete DEA requires that one such linear program be solved for each DMU. The result is both the set of weights for the DMU and the measure of its relative efficiency. Thus, there are no more computational difficulties associated with computing the input and output weights and the efficiencies in DEA than there are in performing the comparable regression analysis to estimate productive efficiencies. (The reader who is generally unfamiliar with linear programming theory and application can consult Hillier and Lieberman, 1986.)

As Chapters Two and Three in this volume demonstrate, the results of a DEA can be of significant managerial value in three important ways. First, DEA produces the efficiency of each DMU relative to all other DMUs in the sample. This measure allows the analyst to identify the DMUs that are in greatest need of attention and the extent to which improvements might be possible, and it enables managers and regulators to focus their attention on the DMUs that the DEA indicates are the least efficient.

Second, whenever a DMU is less than perfectly efficient, DEA indicates a subset of perfectly efficient DMUs (we will call this the *efficient reference set*) and a set of associated multipliers that can be used to formulate managerial strategies for improvement. The resulting information permits the analyst to construct a hypothetical DMU that uses less of each input than, while producing at least as much of each output as, the inefficient DMU and that would be rated perfectly efficient if it used the same input and output weights as the inefficient DMU. This leads naturally to highly specific managerial strategies for improving the efficiency of an inefficient DMU by indicating which inputs are being overutilized, which outputs are being underproduced, and in each case by how much. Thus, not only does management know which DMUs to focus on, it also knows by how much each input and output level needs to be adjusted at each site so as to make the site like its efficient peers.

Third, DEA provides a matrix of cross-efficiencies. The cross-efficiency of DMU A as measured by DMU B is simply the ratio of weighted output to weighted input calculated using the input and output level of DMU A and the input and output weights of DMU B. A careful analysis of cross-efficiencies can help to identify DMUs that are efficient but that use a mixture of inputs and produce a mixture of outputs that are very different from those of most other DMUs. Such DMUs can be viewed as mavericks. Analysis of cross-efficiencies can also be accompanied by a cluster analysis of the input and output weights themselves.

A secondary analysis following the DEA proper involves formulating a model to explain the variation in efficiency among the DMUs in terms of the various statistics that describe them. In the case of the nursing homes, for example, we might want to consider such factors as ownership (proprietary public, not-for-profit), area of operation (urban, suburban, rural), and age of facility as independent variables. The efficiency of the nursing home is the dependent variable. Analysis of covariance is then used to estimate the model parameters. Software for this purpose is available on many mainframe computers. Analysis of covariance is a generalized type of multiple regression that permits categorical as well as interval variables. The residual inefficiency that remains after such an analysis is then assumed to lie within the production process itself, since it cannot be attributed to measured conditions at the DMU. These and other extensions to the basic DEA methodology are discussed in detail in Chapter Four.

A Graphical Approach to DEA

Before we proceed to the linear programming formulation of the DEA model, it will be instructive to examine a small problem graphically. This will help us to visualize the concepts underlying DEA and to interpret the results of DEA in larger problems.

Let us suppose that we are to analyze three DMUs—call them 1, 2, and 3. Each DMU uses two inputs to produce a single output. These DMUs and their input and output levels are illustrated schematically in Figure 1. Because there is only one output, it is reasonable to re-express

Figure 1. Input and Output Levels for the Three DMUs

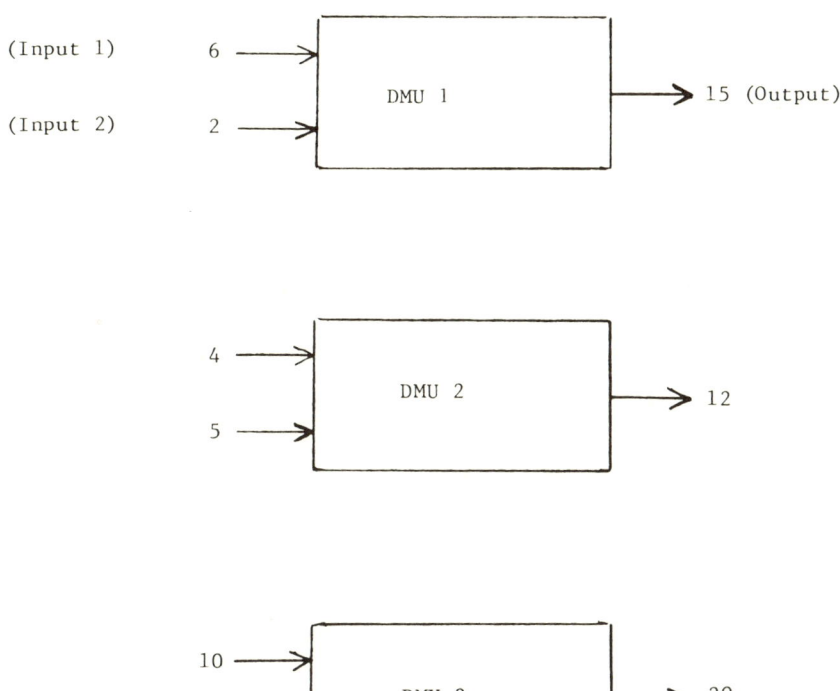

each input level as input per unit output, that is, to divide each input level at a given DMU by the output level of that DMU. The results of these calculations are shown in Table 1. This has the effect of normalizing the input levels of the DMUs and of making it possible for us to compare the normalized input levels across DMUs.

The next step is to plot the normalized input levels of the DMUs, as in Figure 2. In this figure, each DMU is represented by a point whose coordinates are its normalized input levels. In principle, any DMU that is lower than and to the left of another DMU is more efficient that that DMU, because it is producing the same unit of output but is using lower levels of both inputs. It follows that we may view the origin as the ultimate goal toward which all DMUs strive as they attempt to become more efficient.

Figure 2 also shows the so-called efficient frontier for the three DMUs. Every DMU is either on the efficient frontier, or else the line segment between the DMU and the origin crosses the frontier. The efficient

Table 1. Normalized Input Levels for the Three DMUs

Normalized Input Levels

DMU	Input 1/Output			Input 2/Output		
1	6/15	=	0.400	2/15	=	0.133
2	4/12	=	0.333	5/12	=	0.417
3	10/20	=	0.500	8/20	=	0.400

Figure 2. Graph of Normalized Input Levels and the Efficient Frontier for the Three DMUs

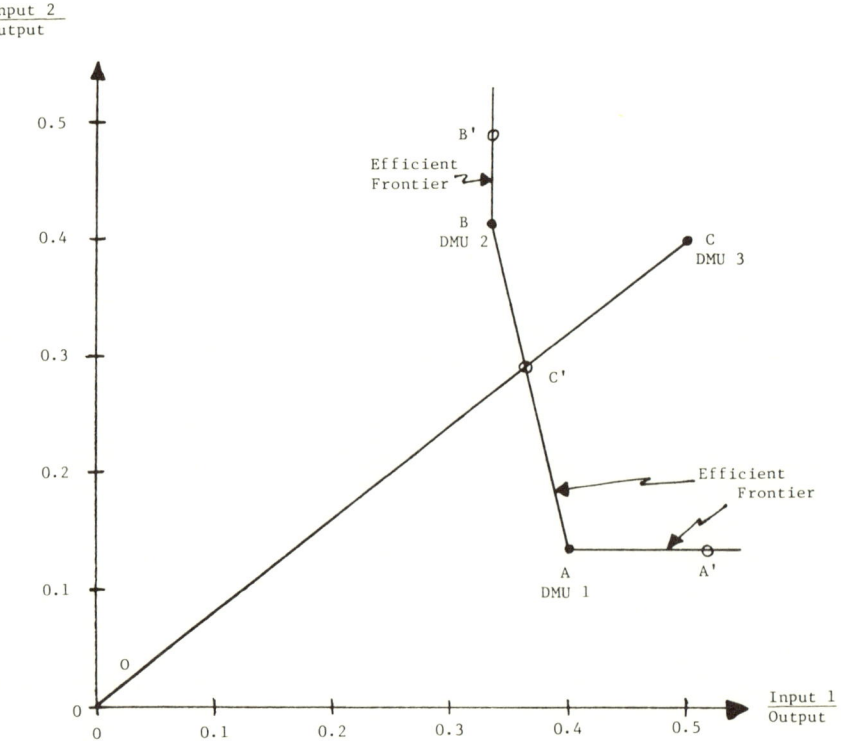

frontier is the piecewise linear curve that is as far up and to the right as possible while still satisfying the condition just stated, that is, it is the lower envelope of the DMUs in the sample.

We can visualize the physical construction of the efficient frontier as follows: Imagine a very long string lying atop the horizontal axis. Now, slide the string upward, keeping it parallel to the horizontal axis, until it contacts one of the plotted points (point *A* corresponding to DMU 1 in our example). Now, keeping the portion of the string to the right of the contact point horizontal, raise the portion to the left so that the string pivots on the contact point. Continue until either the left portion of the string is vertical or another point is touched. In our example, the left portion of the string will contact point *B* corresponding to DMU 2. Whenever a new point is touched, it becomes the new pivot point. The process continues until the left portion of the string is vertical. The final position of the string defines the efficient frontier for the particular set of points. The efficient frontier surrounds the data points corresponding to the DMUs, and it is this image that gives data envelopment analysis its name.

We can now define the efficiency of a DMU in terms of its position relative to the efficient frontier. We can use point *C* corresponding to DMU 3 to illustrate: Construct the line segment between the origin and point *C*. Notice that this line segment crosses the efficient frontier; call the crossing point *C'*. The efficiency of DMU 3 is then equal to the ratio of the length of line segment *OC'* to the length of line segment *OC*. We will say that a DMU is efficient if its efficiency ratio equals one, that is, if the DMU lies on the frontier.

We observe that this definition is reasonable in the following sense: If a DMU lies on the efficient frontier, then the ratio just defined equals one, and the DMU is labeled efficient. If a DMU lies above and to the right of the frontier, then its ratio is less than one. Moreover, the point *C'* corresponds to a hypothetical DMU whose input mixture ratio is the same as that of DMU 3. That is, if there existed a DMU whose normalized input levels corresponded to point *C'*, then its ratio of input level 1 to input level 2 would exactly match that of DMU 3. We might express this by saying that the hypothetical DMU and DMU 3 effectively use the same production technology. Therefore, the hypothetical DMU can be used as a role model toward which DMU 3 should move in its attempt to become more efficient.

We can view this hypothetical DMU in another way. Because point *C'* lies on the line segment between points *A* and *B*, its coordinates are a weighted average of the coordinates of points *A* and *B*. (This is a standard result in geometry.) In this sense, the hypothetical DMU for DMU 3 is a weighted average of DMUs 1 and 2, so we say that DMUs 1 and 2 form the efficient reference set for DMU 3. Clearly, only efficient DMUs can be in the efficient reference set for an inefficient DMU.

In analyzing DMUs in this way, we make a number of assumptions that should be discussed. First, in using a piecewise linear frontier, we are assuming that hypothetical DMUs like those just constructed are in fact feasible. This means that we assume the continuous substitutability of one input for the other in such a way that all points along each line segment on the frontier could actually be achieved. This assumption is questionable when there are only a small number of production technologies from which to choose and where such weighted averages have no counterpart in reality. Alternatively, a point such as C' can be thought of as a DMU that uses the technology of DMU 1 for a certain percentage of the time and the technology of DMU 2 for the rest of the time, where the relative proportions are determined by the weights in the linear combination.

Second, notice that the frontier always extends horizontally to the right from the lowest DMU in the plot of normalized input levels. In Figure 2, imagine a DMU whose normalized input levels corresponded to point A'. By our definition, this DMU would be efficient. But, notice that, while its normalized level of input 2 matches that of DMU 1, its normalized level of input 1 is higher. Such a DMU should not be considered efficient. This anomaly can be avoided by a redefinition of the efficient frontier. The right portion of the frontier is replaced by the line segment connecting the lowest point to a point on the horizontal axis at infinity. The result is that the lowest segment of the efficient frontier now slopes downward very slightly and that the DMU corresponding to point A' in Figure 2 is no longer on the efficient frontier.

The same difficulty exists with the vertical portion of the frontier where a DMU corresponding to point B' in Figure 2 would also be labeled efficient. The solution is the same: Replace the vertical portion of the frontier by the line segment connecting the leftmost point to a point very far up on the vertical axis, essentially a point at infinity. The leftmost segment of the efficient frontier now tilts slightly toward the vertical axis, and the DMU corresponding to point B' is no longer on the efficient frontier.

All efficiency values measured in this way are relative to the set of DMUs under evaluation. If we were to delete some DMU on the frontier from the analysis, then the efficiency scores of many of the remaining DMUs might change. For example, in Figure 2, the deletion of DMU 1 would cause the efficiency of DMU 3 to jump to one. But, while the elimination of DMU 2 would raise the efficiency of DMU 3, it would still not permit point C to be part of the frontier. Of course, the deletion of DMU 3 has no effect. Similar comments apply if DMUs are added to the analysis: If these DMUs become part of the frontier, other DMUs may have their efficiency scores altered. If they do not, there will be no effect. Finally, the scores can change if a DMU on the frontier alters its normalized input levels and thereby moves to a new position.

Measuring efficiency in this manner in no way considers the relative importance of the inputs. In our example, DMU 1 uses relatively more of input 1 than of input 2, while the reverse is true for DMU 2; both DMUs are efficient. But, suppose that input 1 is scarce and that input 2 is abundant. Then, from a broader viewpoint, DMU 2 performs better than DMU 1 does. If there were prices on the inputs, then economic theory predicts that input 1 would be expensive relative to input 2 and that DMU 2 would be identified as a minimum cost producer. But, in DEA applications, such prices are assumed either not to exist or to be irrelevant in measuring efficiency, and therefore no such distinction can be made. This point is discussed in Chapter Four, which makes a distinction between price and technical efficiency. DEA concerns itself with technical efficiency.

The DEA Formulation

The preceding section illustrated the DEA technique graphically for the case in which there are only two inputs and one output. Unfortunately, such procedures cannot work when there are more than three quantities involved, as there are in virtually all applications. In these situations, we require a computationally tractable analytical technique that accomplishes the necessary measurements. For this we turn to a mathematical programming formulation of the problem, which this section describes. Where possible, I will make connections with the graphical analysis.

I begin by describing the decision variables and constants in the model. Suppose that there are n DMUs to be analyzed, each of which uses m inputs to produce s outputs. Let $X_{ij} > 0$ be the amount of input i used by DMU j; let $Y_{rj} > 0$ be the amount of output r produced by DMU j. The decision variables of the problem are the unit weights to be attached to each of the inputs and outputs by DMU k. Let v_{ik} be the unit weight placed on input i by DMU k; let u_{rk} be the unit weight placed on output r by DMU k. We then formulate n fractional linear programs, one for each of the n DMUs in the set. The objective function of the fractional linear program is the ratio of the total weighted output of DMU k divided by its total weighted input:

$$\text{Maximize } h_k = \frac{\sum_{r=1}^{s} u_{rk} Y_{rk}}{\sum_{i=1}^{m} v_{ik} X_{ik}}$$

The universality criterion requires DMU k to choose these weights subject to the constraint that no other DMU would have an efficiency greater than one if it used the same weights:

$$\frac{\sum_{r=1}^{s} u_{rk} Y_{rj}}{\sum_{i=1}^{m} v_{ik} X_{ij}} \leq 1 \; ; j = 1, \ldots, n$$

Also, the selected weights cannot be negative:

$$u_{rk} \geq 0; r = 1, \ldots, s$$

$$v_{ik} \geq 0; i = 1, \ldots, m$$

Some authors require the variables to be strictly positive. Doing so guarantees that DMUs corresponding to points like A' and B' in Figure 2 will not be perfectly efficient. However, we are not likely to encounter such cases in applications, and the strict positivity requirement complicates the analysis without providing much real benefit. Consequently, I shall ignore it.

The fractional linear program is then transformed into an ordinary linear program, and the simplex method is used to solve it. The transformed linear program, which we will call (DEA), is:

(DEA) Maximize $h_k = \sum_{r=1}^{s} u_{rk} Y_{rk}$

subject to

$$[p_{kj}] \quad \sum_{r=1}^{s} u_{rk} Y_{rj} - \sum_{i=1}^{m} v_{ik} X_{ij} \leq 0 \; ; j = 1, \ldots, n$$

$$[q_k] \quad \sum_{i=1}^{m} v_{ik} X_{ik} = 1$$

$$u_{rk} \geq 0 \; ; r = 1, \ldots, s$$
$$v_{ik} \geq 0 \; ; i = 1, \ldots, m$$

The dual variables, which are shown in square brackets, will be used later in this chapter. A complete DEA involves the solution of n such linear programs, one for each DMU. These linear programs are very similar one to another; they differ only in the objective function coefficients and in the coefficients of the last constraints. (As a result, it is possible to reduce the computational effort needed to solve the DEA problem substantially by invoking the methods of linear programming sensitivity analysis so that the final tableau corresponding to the first DMU can be modified and used as the initial tableau for the second DMU and so forth.) In most practical situations, these linear programs will be small; each has $m + s$ decision variables, the number of inputs plus outputs—usually no more than ten—and $n+1$ constraints—perhaps a few hundred at most. Even personal computers have the capacity to solve such problems.

Example

Let us illustrate the preceding ideas with an example. Consider the set of six nursing homes whose inputs and outputs for a given year are described in Table 2. *StHr* stands for staff hours per day, including nurses, physicians, therapists, and so forth. *Supp* stands for supplies per day, which are measured in thousands of dollars. *MCPD* stands for total Medicare- plus Medicaid-reimbursed patient days, and *PPPD* stands for total privately paid patient days. Thus, the inputs are measured on a daily basis, while the outputs are annual totals. This is strictly for the sake of convenience. We could have expressed all inputs and outputs in the same units, but this is unnecessary, since the basic DEA formulation assumes constant returns to scale.

Table 3 shows the results of a standard ratio analysis on these data. I have computed the ratio of each output to each input for each DMU and shown the rank of each DMU within each ratio. Some features are immediately apparent. For instance, DMU A rates highest in MCPD/Supp but lowest in PPPD/StHr, while DMU B rates highest in PPPD/Supp but lowest in MCPD/StHr. In fact, each of the first four DMU rates highest in one ratio and lowest in another. Meanwhile, DMUs E and F occupy each of the intermediate ranks exactly once without ever being best or worst on any scale.

Table 2. Inputs and Outputs for the Six Nursing Homes

	Inputs		Outputs	
DMU	StHr	Supp	MCPD	PPPD
A	150	0.2	14000	3500
B	400	0.7	14000	21000
C	320	1.2	42000	10500
D	520	2.0	28000	42000
E	350	1.2	19000	25000
F	320	0.7	14000	15000

Table 3. Ratio Analysis for the Six Nursing Homes

	Ratio			
DMU	MCPD/StHr	PPPD/StHr	MCPD/Supp	PPPD/Supp
A	93.3 (2)	23.3 (6)	70000 (1)	17500 (5)
B	35.0 (6)	52.5 (3)	20000 (3)	30000 (1)
C	131.3 (1)	32.8 (5)	35000 (2)	8750 (6)
D	53.8 (4)	80.8 (1)	14000 (6)	21000 (3)
E	54.3 (3)	71.4 (2)	15833 (5)	20833 (4)
F	43.8 (5)	46.9 (4)	20000 (3)	21429 (2)

Note: The rank of each DMU within each ratio is shown in parentheses.

What does Table 3 say about the relative efficiencies of the six DMUs? The only real conclusion that we can draw seems to be that DMUs A through D are specialists in converting one type of input into one type of output. DMU A uses very little Supp and produces quite a bit of MCPD, relatively speaking. If Supp had been identified as the most valuable input and if MCPD had been identified as the most valuable output, then all nursing homes should be encouraged to behave like DMU A. Corresponding statements apply to DMUs B through D. But, we do not have such value judgments, for if we did, we could use values to evaluate the performance of each DMU, and efficiency measurement would not present any difficulties. So, all we can conclude is that DMUs A through D are specialists, while DMUs E and F operate somewhere away from the extremes. We might agree that DMUs A through D are efficient, but there seems to be no consensus regarding DMUs E and F.

Table 4 presents the results of the multiple regression approach. Recall that the multiple regression approach requires all outputs to be combined into a single measure of production. For these purposes, I have defined *TPD* as total patient days, regardless of reimbursement method. Therefore, TPD is the sum of MCPD and PPPD. To reduce the effects of roundoff error in the regression calculations, TPD is expressed in tens of thousands of patient days, and StHr is expressed in hundreds of hours per day. The multiple regression equation, estimated by the least-squares methods, is

$$TPD = 1.21 - 0.02 \times StHr + 2.98 \times Supp$$

The regression equation is highly statistically significant, with a multiple R-squared of 0.97. The coefficient of Supp is also highly statistically significant, but the coefficient of StHr is not significant at all. Nevertheless, we will leave both variables in the model, since our goal is to achieve prediction accuracy, not to decide which inputs belong and which do not. (That, of course, is an important question in itself. In this case, the deletion of StHr results in a model with similar coefficients that produces almost the same predictions. The model that uses only StHr is statistically significant, but it produces very different estimates, which illustrates the importance of selecting the right variables no matter what approach is used.)

Table 4. Results of the Multiple Regression Analysis for the Six Nursing Homes

DMU	TPD Actual	Estimated	(3)−(2)	(4)÷(3)
A	17500	17800	− 300	− 1.7
B	35000	32300	2700	8.4
C	52500	47300	5200	11.0
D	70000	70800	− 800	− 1.1
E	44000	47300	− 3300	− 7.0
F	29000	32400	− 3400	− 10.5

According to Table 4, DMU C is the most efficient, and DMU F is the least efficient. The multiple regression model predicts that a DMU with StHr = 3.2 and Supp = 1.2 will produce TPD = 4.73 (the regression coefficients have been rounded for clarity). Thus, DMU C would be expected to produce 47,300 patient days. In fact, it produced 52,500, an excess of 5,200 or 11 percent above the prediction. Conversely, the multiple regression model predicts that a DMU with StHr = 3.2 and Supp = 0.7 will produce TPD = 3.24. Thus, DMU F would be expected to produce 32,400 patient days. In fact, it produced 29,000, a shortfall of 3,400 or 10.5 percent below the prediction.

In some respects, the multiple regression analysis has provided somewhat more satisfactory results. We now have a measure of efficiency for each DMU (the percentage of estimated column in Table 4). However, as I pointed out earlier, these scores are relative to a surface representing average, not best possible, performance. In addition, we have had to combine our two outputs into one. It was not difficult to do so in this example, but in another it might have been nearly impossible. How might we combine, for example, average standardized test scores in reading and mathematics for a school? In a hospital application, how might we combine patient days and interns trained? Notice that by combining the outputs we have lost the ability to identify DMUs A through D as specialists. Thus, while we gained something with the multiple regression approach, we also lost something.

Table 5 shows the DEA results for this example. StHr is expressed in hundreds of hours per day, and both MCPD and PPPD are expressed in tens of thousands of patient days. The last column shows the efficiency score, while the first four columns show the weights selected by each DMU. As the ratio analysis suggested, DMUs A through D are perfectly relatively efficient. Moreover, DMU C places all its input weight on StHr and all its output weight on MCPD. In the ratio analysis, DMU C was rated highest in MCPD/StHr. Similar remarks apply to DMU D for StHr and PPPD. However, this phenomenon does not occur with DMUs A and B. This is because, as we shall see in Chapter Four, whenever a DMU is perfectly relatively efficient, its linear program possesses multiple optimal solutions. In this situation, the simplex method reports the first optimal solution that it finds. In the present example, the first solutions found for DMUs A and B happened to put positive weights on both inputs thereby obscuring the fact that the DMUs are specialists. Chapter Four presents a linear goal-programming formulation for DEA that avoids this and other problems.

Table 5. Optimal Weights and Efficiencies from the DEA for the Six Nursing Homes

DMU	Input Weights		Output Weights		Efficiency
	StHr	Supp	MCPD	PPPD	
A	0.517	1.121	0.714	0	1.000
B	0.138	0.642	0	0.476	1.000
C	0.313	0	0.238	0	1.000
D	0.192	0	0	0.238	1.000
E	0.110	0.513	0.115	0.304	0.977
F	0.155	0.722	0.162	0.427	0.867

We now seem to have some definitive results concerning DMUs E and F. No matter what weights they choose, they cannot achieve an efficiency score of one. The best that DMU E can do is 0.977, while the maximum for DMU F is 0.867. Thus, DMUs E and F are inefficient, and DMU F is more inefficient that DMU E. In fact, we can say a good deal more about DMUs E and F. In particular, we can now specify a management strategy indicating by how much each DMU should reduce each input and increase each output in order to become perfectly efficient. To see this, we must first examine the dual of the DEA linear program.

The Dual of the DEA Linear Program

Recall that in our graphical example DMUs 1 and 2 were the efficient reference set for DMU 3. This meant that the hypothetical DMU after which DMU 3 should model itself was in some sense a weighted average of DMUs 1 and 2. It also means that the input and output levels of the hypothetical DMU are linear combinations of the input and output levels of DMUs 1 and 2. The question is, What are the coefficients of that linear combination? In other words, to obtain the output level of the hypothetical DMU, we should add some multiple of the output level of DMU 1 to some multiple of the output level of DMU 2. What multiples should we use?

The answer lies in the solution to the dual of the linear program (DEA). In the theory of linear programming, every linear program has a companion linear program, which is called its *dual*. The dual problem, which uses a completely different set of variables, has its own set of constraints and its own objective function expressed in terms of those variables. There are formal rules for the construction of the dual problem, and there are standard ways of interpreting the values of the dual variables. Moreover, linear programming theory teaches that, when the simplex method is applied to any linear program, not only do we obtain its optimal solution, we also obtain the optimal solution to the dual problem. Thus, with no additional computational effort, whenever we solve the problem (DEA), we also solve its dual; that is, we obtain the values of the dual variables that optimize the dual objective function while satisfying all the dual constraints.

As we will see, the dual problem has one dual variable for each DMU (including itself) and one other. If a DMU is efficient, then its optimal dual solution will have all dual variables equal to zero except for the dual variable corresponding to the DMU itself and the extra dual variable, both of which will equal one. The interesting case occurs if a DMU is inefficient. In such a case, the extra dual variable will equal its efficiency score, while the other dual variables will be the required coefficients in the linear combination just described. Now, some of these dual variables will be zero. In fact, only efficient DMUs can ever be assigned a positive dual variable. Indeed, the set of DMUs to which a positive dual variable is assigned is precisely the efficient reference set defined earlier. In other words, the dual variables identify the efficient reference set for an inefficient DMU and also provide the multipliers needed to produce the input and output levels of the hypothetical DMU.

I now provide some of the details. Let us return to the linear programming formulation that I called (DEA). Recall that the dual variables are given in square brackets. The dual of (DEA), which we will call (Dual), is

(Dual) Minimize $w_k = q_k$

subject to

$$[u_{rk}] \sum_{j=1}^{n} p_{kj} Y_{rj} \geq Y_{rk} \quad r = 1, \ldots, s$$

$$-\sum_{j=1}^{n} p_{kj} X_{ij} + q_k X_{ik} \geq 0 \quad i = 1, \ldots, m$$

$$p_{kj} \geq 0 \quad j = 1, \ldots, n$$

q_k unrestricted in sign

Now, the original primal variables (the input and output weights) are shown in square brackets. As already noted, the simplex method for solving (DEA) also produces the optimal values of the dual variables, so that by solving (DEA) we have also solved (Dual).

The dual problem contains one p variable for each DMU in the set and one q variable, all of which can be meaningfully interpreted to provide important managerial information. The q variable is the simplest to interpret. By linear programming duality theory, the optimal value of q_k equals the optimal value of h_k. Thus, q_k is the efficiency of DMU k. It must lie between zero and one despite the absence of any such formal constraint. Indeed, q_k must be positive, for if q_k were zero, then every p_{kj} would have to be zero in order to satisfy the last m constraints of (Dual). (Recall that each $X_{ij} > 0$.) But, this precludes satisfying the first s constraints of (Dual), because each $Y_{rj} > 0$.

Consider the p variables. By linear programming complementary slackness theory, the optimal value of p_{kj} is positive if and only if the corresponding constraint in (DEA) is satisfied with equality. This implies that DMU j must be efficient. To see this, recognize that DMU j would merely have to select the weights used by DMU k, but appropriately scaled so as to satisfy DMU j's last constraint. Such scaling would not alter any of the first n constraints in DMU j's version of (DEA), and it would give DMU j an efficiency score of one. The set of necessarily efficient DMUs to which DMU k attaches a positive dual variable p_{kj} is, as previously defined, the efficient reference set for DMU k. Generally, if DMU k is efficient, then it will be the only DMU in its efficient reference set, and the corresponding dual variable, p_{kk}, will equal one.

Suppose now that DMU k has an efficiency score less than one. Let us imagine a hypothetical DMU, say DMU O, whose input and output levels are the following linear combinations of the input and output levels of the DMUs in the efficient reference set of DMU k:

$$X_{io} = \sum_{j \in E_k} p_{kj} X_{ij} \qquad i = 1, \ldots, m$$

$$Y_{ro} = \sum_{j \in E_k} p_{kj} Y_{rj} \qquad r = 1, \ldots, s$$

There are two remarkable features of DMU O. First, it dominates DMU k in that it uses strictly less of each input than DMU k while producing at least as much of each output. This is easily seen from the constraints of the dual, keeping in mind that q_k is the efficiency of DMU k and that, because we have assumed that DMU k is inefficient, it must be strictly less than one. Second, DMU O is itself efficient, and its optimal input and output weights are proportional to those selected by DMU k. (The constant of proportionality is $1/q_k$.) To see this, consider the efficiency ratio of DMU O using the input and output weights produced by DMU k:

$$\frac{\sum_{r=1}^{s} u_{rk} Y_{ro}}{\sum_{i=1}^{m} v_{ik} X_{io}} = \frac{\sum_{r=1}^{s} u_{rk} \left(\sum_{j \in E_k} p_{kj} Y_{rj} \right)}{\sum_{i=1}^{m} v_{ik} \left(\sum_{j \in E_k} p_{kj} X_{ij} \right)} = \frac{\sum_{j \in E_k} p_{kj} \left(\sum_{r=1}^{s} u_{rk} Y_{rj} \right)}{\sum_{j \in E_k} p_{kj} \left(\sum_{r=1}^{m} v_{ik} X_{ij} \right)} = 1$$

The first step substitutes the definitions of X_{io} and Y_{ro}. The second step interchanges the summation signs. The identification of the numerator and denominator in the last step follows from the observation from (DEA) for DMU k that the expressions in parentheses must be equal whenever p_{kj} is positive; that is, DMU j is in the efficient reference set for DMU k. All that remains is for DMU O to scale the input and output weights so as to satisfy the last constraint in its version of (DEA). That $1/q_k$ is the appropriate scaling factor follows from

$$\sum_{i=1}^{m} v_{ik} X_{io} = \sum_{i=1}^{m} v_{ik} \left(q_k X_{ik} \right)$$

$$= q_k \sum_{i=1}^{m} v_{ik} X_{ik} = q_k$$

The first step replaces X_{io} with $q_k X_{ik}$. While it is false when $v_{ik} = 0$, no harm is done by the substitution, since the product $v_{ik} X_{io}$ vanishes in this case anyway. The second step factors out the term q_k. The third step follows from the feasibility of the v_{ik} in (DEA) for DMU k.

Thus, the dual variables permit us to construct a hypothetical DMU that is perfectly efficient and that dominates DMU k. This hypothetical DMU is a linear combination of the DMUs in the efficient reference set for DMU k. Therefore, as noted earlier, the efficient reference set for DMU k can be thought of as a set of role models, and the hypothetical DMU in some sense represents a single site that DMU k should try to imitate. Such imitation requires DMU k to reduce all inputs by at least $(1 - q_k) * 100$ (more for those inputs for which v_{ik} equals zero) and simultaneously increase all outputs for which u_{rk} equals zero.

Thus, the dual produces precisely the sort of managerial information needed in order to put the results of an efficiency analysis to good use: It tells the analyst exactly how each inefficient DMU should adjust itself to become efficient. And, while there are infinitely many ways in which an inefficient DMU can become efficient (any place on the frontier will do), the dual provides the unique way in which the DMU does not need to alter its relative mixes of inputs and outputs, only their individual levels. No input would ever be increased and no output would ever be decreased in the strategy proposed by the dual, a feature of clear intuitive appeal.

The Dual in the Example

Recall that in our example DMUs A through D are efficient but that DMUs E and F have efficiency values of 0.977 and 0.867, respectively. As we would expect from the discussion in the last section, we find that the solutions for DMUs A through D have $p_{11} = p_{22} = p_{33} = p_{44} = 1$; all other dual variables are equal to zero. We find also that DMU E has three DMUs in its efficient reference set: DMUs A, B, and D. (Of course, only efficient DMUs can appear in any efficient reference set.) The dual variables for the DMUs are 0.2, 0.08, and 0.538, respectively. Notice that, even though we use the dual variables as multipliers, they do not need to sum to one.

The hypothetical DMU for DMU E—call it DMU E'—has input and output levels that are 0.2 times those for DMU A plus 0.08 times those for DMU B plus 0.538 times those for DMU D. This turns out (refer to Table 2) to be StHr = 342, Supp = 1.17, MCPD = 19,000, and PPPD = 25,000, where I have rounded off somewhat along the way. (Since DMU E places positive weight on both inputs and both outputs, as Table 5 shows, we could simply have reduced each input by $(1 - 0.977) * 100 = 2.3$ percent and kept each output constant. Generally, only those inputs and outputs with zero weight need to be computed.) Thus, to imitate DMU E', DMU E should try to reduce each input level by 2.3 percent without lowering either output level. The reader can verify that DMU E′ is efficient when it uses the input and output weights produced by DMU E (refer again to Table 5), provided, of course, that StHr, MCPD, and PPPD are expressed in the units used when (DEA) was solved.

Very similar remarks apply to DMU F. Its efficient reference set also contains DMUs A, B, and D, but the dual variables are shifted toward DMUs A and B and away from DMU D. The values of the dual variables are 0.343, 0.395, and 0.131 for the DMUs A, B, and D, respectively. We could compute the input and output levels for its hypothetical DMU, DMU F′, but since DMU F places a positive weight on each input and output (refer to Table 5), it is easier to reduce each of DMU F's inputs by $(1 - 0.8367) * 100 = 13.3$ percent and leave each of its outputs unchanged. This gives DMU F′ StHr = 278, Supp = 0.607, MCPD = 14,000, and PPPD = 15,000 (all in original units).

These results contrast interestingly with those suggested by the multiple regression approach. There, we decided that DMU C seemed to be most efficient (refer to Table 4), because it was 11 percent above its predicted output levels which was more above its predicted output level than any other DMU in percentage terms. Here, we notice that DMU C is the only efficient DMU that does not appear in any efficient reference set. By this measure, DMU C is the worst of the four efficient DMUs, and DMU D is the best. The multiple regression analysis indicated that DMU D was below par, because it produced 1.1 percent less than the level predicted by the model. Chapter Four discusses another indicator of efficiency that helps to differentiate among efficient DMUs. Chapter Four will conclude that DMU D is superior to DMU C but that DMU A might be better still.

In most situations, the results of such an analysis must be converted into cost savings. In our example, this is actually simple. Let us assume an average wage rate, including fringe benefits, of $30 per hour, strictly for purposes of illustration. In reducing StHr by 8 per day, DMU E saves $240 per day on labor. In reducing StHr by 42 per day, DMU F saves $1,260 per day. Now, Supp is expressed in thousands of dollars per day, so, in reducing Supp by 0.03, DMU E saves $30 per day on supplies, and, in reducing Supp by 0.093, DMU F saves $93 per day. The total cost savings for DMUs E and F, then, are $270 per day and $1,353 per day, respectively, and the grand total is $1,623 per day.

Limitations of DEA

To be sure, DEA has some limitations, but these are both less numerous and less severe than those of other techniques. First, DEA requires all inputs and outputs to be specified and measured, as do ratio analysis and multiple regression analysis—and indeed, any efficiency-measuring procedure. Failure to include a valid input or output will bias the results against efficient users of the input or efficient producers of the output. Inclusion of an invalid input or output causes some DMUs to be rated as more efficient than they really are. Thus, like any other type of analysis, DEA must be properly structured.

Second, DEA assumes that each unit of a given input or output is identical to all other units of the same type. In a hospital application in which nursing labor is disaggregated by skill level on the input side, DEA assumes that each hour of labor provided by a registered nurse is equivalent to any other hour provided by any other registered nurse. In fact, one nurse may be more experienced or better trained than another and therefore take less time to perform a given nursing task. On the output side, DEA assumes that each patient day produced at hospital A is identical to each patient day produced at hospital B (even controlling for severity of illness) while in fact there may be differences of a type that involves the quality of care. Unless these differences can be measured—and experience indicates that they cannot—DEA will be biased in favor of the hospital at which quality is lower if it saves resources or increases outputs as a result. However, this problem is inherent in the data base, not in the technique, and it pervades all efficiency analyses regardless of method.

Third, in its basic form, DEA assumes constant returns to scale. That is, proportional changes in all input levels result in changes of equal proportion in output levels. This is an important assumption, since it allows all DMUs to be scaled and compared to a unit isoquant. The same frontier or production surface is thus applicable to all DMUs. Ratio analysis and multiple regression analysis share the same limitation if a linear surface is assumed, as is often the case. However, recent research (Byrnes and others, 1984) indicates that DEA can be used to detect and measure scale effects.

Fourth, the input and output weights produced by DEA cannot be interpreted as values in the economic sense even though they seem to share the same mathematical representation. In fact, the optimal weights for a given DMU often include zeroes when no one would argue that the corresponding entities are valueless. However, this is not so much a shortcoming of the procedure as it is a caveat bearing on interpretation of the results. DEA does not purport to ascertain the unit values of inputs and outputs, only to measure relative efficiency.

References

Bessent, A., Bessent, W., Kennington, J., and Reagan, B. "An Application of Mathematical Programming to Assess Productivity in the Houston Independent School District." *Management Science*, 1982, *28* (12), 1355-1367.

Byrnes, P., Fare, R., and Grosskopf, S. "Measuring Productive Efficiency: An Application to Illinois Strip Mines." *Management Science*, 1984, *30* (6), 671-681.

Charnes, A., Cooper, W. W., and Rhodes, E. "Measuring the Efficiency of Decision-Making Units." *European Journal of Operational Research,* 1978, *2* (6), 429-444.

Charnes, A., Cooper, W. W., and Rhodes, E. "Measuring the Efficiency of Decision-Making Units: Short Communication." *European Journal of Operational Research,* 1979, *3* (4), 339.

Charnes, A., Cooper, W. W., and Rhodes, E. "Evaluating Program and Managerial Efficiency: An Application of Data Envelopment Analysis to Program Follow Through." *Management Science,* 1981, *27* (6), 668-697.

Fare, R., and Primont, D. "Efficiency Measures for Multiplant Firms." *Operations Research Letters,* 1984, *3* (5), 257-260.

Forsund, F. R., Knox-Lovell, C. A., and Schmidt, P. "A Survey of Frontier Production Functions and of Their Relationship to Efficiency Measurement." *Journal of Econometrics,* 1980, *13,* 5-25.

Hillier, F. S., and Lieberman, G. J. *Introduction to Operations Research.* (4th ed.) Oakland, Calif.: Holden-Day, 1986.

Lewin, A. Y., Morey, R. C., and Cook, T. J. "Evaluating the Administrative Efficiency of Courts." *Omega,* 1982, *10* (4), 401-426.

Nunamaker, T. R. "Measuring Routine Nursing Service Efficiency: A Comparison of Cost Per Patient Day and Data Envelopment Analysis Models." *Health Services Research,* 1983, *18* (2), 183-205.

Rhodes, E. L. *A Study of U.S. National Park Service Performance Variations: An Application of Data Envelopment Analysis.* Working Paper Series No. 531. Buffalo: School of Management, State University of New York, 1982.

Sherman, H. D. "Hospital Efficiency Measurement and Evaluation: Empirical Test of a New Technique." *Medical Care,* 1984, *22* (10), 922-938.

Thomas R. Sexton is associate professor in the W. Averell Harriman College for Policy Analysis and Public Management, the State University of New York at Stony Brook.

Improving the efficiency and reducing the cost of health care is a particularly complex task. DEA can be used to identify real hospital inefficiencies and opportunities for cost reduction that more traditional techniques do not reveal.

Managing Productivity of Health Care Organizations

H. David Sherman

Health care encompasses numerous services that need to be managed through cooperation of management and health care professionals—physicians, nurses, therapists, and so forth. The health care professional's judgment determines the type of care, amount of care, period of care, and location of treatment. Professional judgment is a key influence over the resources used and costs incurred by hospitals, labs, and other providers in treating a patient, and health care professionals differ in their judgments, just as other professionals do. Consequently, it is difficult to develop standard procedures and treatments for a given illness. Different physicians may prescribe different numbers of tests, different treatments, or different periods of treatment for the same illness.

The absence of standards for health care services raises questions about how we are to evaluate whether a health care provider uses excessive resources in the treatment of patients. The situation is complicated by the numerous types of illnesses that are treated. Data envelopment analysis (DEA) offers some useful tools for the evaluation of resource management among health care providers. The use of DEA for this purpose has a number of potential benefits.

Health care costs represent a substantial part of corporate and government expenditures, and for the last ten years these costs have grown at a rate that exceeds the rate of inflation. Hence, health care in itself represents a significant industry that has widespread impact on our society. Cost containment in this industry has become a key concern of business and government. If the sole contribution that DEA could make was to increase efficiency in the health care industry, it would be a highly valued tool. This chapter addresses the application of DEA to acute care hospitals. Successful use of DEA in acute care hospitals would suggest that it could also be applied to rehabilitation hospitals, nursing homes, health maintenance organizations, and freestanding clinics. Preferred provider organizations (PPOs), which select particular hospitals to provide care to a particular patient group, might also be able to use DEA to identify relatively inefficient hospitals as ineligible for consideration for PPO contracts. If DEA were used in this way, only more efficient, lower-cost hospitals could be included in the plan. DEA could also be used by Medicare, Medicaid, and other programs that establish reimbursement rates for health services to their constituencies. Reimbursement rates have tended to be based on historical averages, which reflect the costs both of more- and less-efficient organizations. If DEA were used to identify the inefficient units, these rates could be based only on the more-efficient units.

New prospective reimbursement mechanisms, such as the diagnosis-related groups (DRG) that Medicare is now using to pay for patients' hospital care, set fees for each category of illness treated. This approach provides incentives to prevent a hospital from becoming less efficient (Bentley and Butler, 1980; Biles and others, 1980; General Accounting Office, 1980). However, these mechanisms do not assure that hospitals will become more efficient, partly because strategies aimed at maximizing reimbursement may not serve to improve efficiency and partly because prospective reimbursement systems are based largely on current cost levels, which are not necessarily the most efficient cost levels. That is, prospective systems may only motivate a hospital to limit the rate of cost increases from an already inefficient cost level. Hence, other, more direct approaches to the improvement of hospital efficiency are needed as one means of reducing health care costs.

Numerous studies (for example, Feldstein, 1968) have attempted to use regression techniques to identify the efficient hospital production relationships. These studies share a common methodological weakness in that they use data that include both efficient and inefficient hospitals to estimate average input-output relationships. These studies may provide good predictions of what costs will be assuming a constant level of inefficiency, but they say nothing about efficient relationships (Bowlin and others, 1985; Sherman, 1982). Other studies have used extremal econometric techniques to estimate efficient, rather than mean, relationships. A review of these efforts by Forsund and others (1980) suggests that these techniques have not yet reached a state of development that allows them to be used to estimate the efficient production function even of simple organizations that produce only one output.

The General Accounting Office (1980) study of U.S. hospitals indicated that a large percentage lacked a number of good management practices that represent key ways of assuring operating efficiency. The GAO study suggested that implementation of improved management practices would result in cost savings without a sacrifice in the quality or quantity of care provided. Hence, there appears to be much potential for improvements in hospital productivity, and new techniques that could be used to assist in this process would be welcome.

Efficiency Measurement Techniques Commonly Applied to Hospitals

Two approaches are widespread in the evaluation of hospital efficiency. Ratio analysis has been used to locate relationships that are abnormally high or abnormally low for such factors as cost per patient day, cost per patient, and personnel full-time equivalents (FTEs) per patient for a group of comparable hospitals. Econometric regression techniques have been used to estimate hospital cost relationships and production relationships. Feldstein (1968) typifies this approach, which attempts to estimate marginal cost per patient, to break down fixed and variable costs, and to identify economies of scale and rates of substitution between inputs.

Ratio Analysis. Ratio analysis calculates and attempts to understand the relationship between two variables, such as cost per day or cost per patient. By its nature, each ratio is limited to one output and one input, and it cannot easily accommodate situations in which multiple inputs are used to produce multiple outputs. Assume, for example, that a hospital treats only two types of patients and that it also trains residents. This hospital would have three outputs. Assume also that cost per patient day is calculated as total number of patient days/total costs. This ratio would be biased because the calculation does not recognize that two different types of patients are being treated and because it ignores the training outputs. Hence, if the cost per patient day was relatively high, it could be due to the case mix, to the intensity of training activity, to excessive prices paid for resources used, or to excessive amounts of resources used.

The problem would be partly remedied if the efficient relative weights or costs for each type of patient care and for each other type of output were available. Unfortunately, these efficient relative weights are not known for most hospital services because it is difficult to agree upon the amount of direct labor and materials required to provide efficient care for a particular diagnosis and because it is even more difficult to establish the way in which joint costs should be allocated among various services. Another problem with the use of ratios to compare hospitals is that ratios offer no objective way of pinpointing inefficient hospitals. Typically, hospitals with cost per patient or cost per day some distance above the mean might be considered potentially inefficient (Hospital Bureau, Massachusetts Rate Setting Commission, 1980). However, there is currently no way of determining how far above the mean is inefficient or even whether the mean is efficient. It is conceivable that all hospitals operating at the mean cost per patient day are also inefficient.

To compensate for the unidimensionality of a single ratio, large sets of ratios have been developed, as in Monitrend reports. One hospital may appear to be relatively efficient on one group of ratios and inefficient on another group of ratios. Another hospital may have the opposite result for the same ratios. There is no objective way of assigning relative weights to these ratios. Consequently, it is difficult to conclude which hospitals are inefficient from ratio analysis.

However, ratio analysis is very useful in identifying the aspects of a hospital's operations that are out of line with the norm. The appeal of ratio analysis is that it relies on simple mathematical concepts and that it can be useful in locating extremely good or extremely poor operating relationships if interpreted in light of the limitations outlined here.

Regression Analysis. Regression analysis is more comprehensive than ratio analysis because it can accommodate multiple outputs and inputs. However, it has a number of significant problems of its own. First, the use of least-squares regression techniques results in estimates of average (or central tendency) relationships, which are not necessarily efficient relationships. Regression techniques reflect efficient relationships only when all the observations themselves are efficient (Sherman, 1981, 1982; Bowlin and others, 1985). Regression techniques have been justified in industry studies, where profit maximization is believed to motivate all firms to operate at or near the efficient production frontiers. The same assumption cannot be made for hospitals (General Accounting Office, 1980).

Second, an estimate of the hospital cost function by means of regression techniques results in a mean relationship, which does not directly locate inefficient hospitals. In order to designate certain hospitals as relatively inefficient, we must label hospitals with costs some arbitrary distance from the mean as potentially inefficient. More important, numerous regression-based hospital studies have been used to identify economies of scale, marginal costs of patient care, and rates of substitution among outputs and inputs. These results say nothing about efficient rates of substitution, efficient scale size, and efficient rates of transformation, because they reflect the behavior of efficient and inefficient hospitals combined. Use of regression techniques would provide insights into efficient hospital behavior only if all hospitals in the study were known to be efficient. While this problem was noted early on by Feldstein (1968), econometric regression techniques are among the most accessible, and they have consequently been widely used in hospital industry studies. Econometric regression techniques are very effectively used in understanding characteristics that have an impact on cost. For example, Feldstein's study (1968) was among the first to measure the sizable impact that case mix has on hospital costs.

Data Envelopment Analysis. Data envelopment analysis addresses the limitations associated with ratio analysis and regression techniques. Data envelopment analysis can accommodate both the case mix—that is, the hundreds of diagnosis types treated in a hospital—and the multiple resources used to produce these services in order to gain an overall picture of a hospital's technical efficiency. In addition, it can incorporate other hospital outputs, such as teaching, research, and community education programs, to gain a comprehensive measure of the efficiency of hospital performance.

Using DEA to Evaluate the Efficiency of Teaching Hospitals

A set of teaching hospitals in Massachusetts was used to assess the ability of DEA to identify relatively inefficient hospitals. No accepted rating system was available that independently indicated which of the hospitals in this set were more or less efficient. In lieu of an absolute benchmark of efficiency, a panel of hospital experts that included regulators, managers, and hospital management consultants familiar with hospitals in the state was enlisted to identify the outputs and inputs that were relevant for the efficiency evaluation and to evaluate the accuracy of the DEA results. The procedures the panel followed are described in greater detail in Sherman (1981) and simulated in Sherman (1984).

Choice of Sample. The Massachusetts Rate Setting Commission (1980) and its Hospital Bureau (1980) had already adopted a ratio analysis approach to the evaluation of hospitals whereby a hospital that was more than one standard deviation above the mean cost per day or mean cost per patient was deemed to be potentially inefficient. This ratio analysis approach was applied within groups of hospitals that were designated as comparable groups. The rate-setting commission used cluster analysis modified by discussion with the hospitals to develop these comparable groups. One of these comparable groups of hospitals, a set of teaching hospitals, was selected for the study described in this chapter, and the data used for the study were obtained from the annual reports that each hospital in the state is required to submit to the rate-setting commission (Massachusetts Rate Setting Commission, 1978). Data were available for seven of the nine hospitals in the group of teaching hospitals, so the DEA was used to evaluate those seven hospitals. The study focused on a single part of each hospital, the medical-surgical area, so that the nature of any inefficiencies that were identified could be verified and explored in depth and so that DEA could be tested in detail. The medical-surgical area was selected because it represented the largest single cost area separately reported on by hospitals in the state. Of course, DEA is applicable to other departments and to the assessment of efficiency for entire hospitals.

The actual data used are included in Table 1. While there are obvious differences in the size and volume of activity among the seven hospitals, they are all considerably smaller than other teaching hospitals in Massachusetts, they all are considered to have a relatively complicated case mix due to their teaching orientation, and they all provide medical education services in addition to patient care. Hence, the hospitals in this set can be considered to be a comparable group.

Identification of Relevant Outputs and Inputs. A key ingredient in a DEA evaluation involves the identification and measurement of relevant inputs and outputs. The advantage of DEA over other techniques is that each input and output can be measured in its natural physical units; there is no need for a weighting system that collapses these different units into dollars or any other single unit measure. Hence, it is sufficient to know, for example, how many patients of each diagnosis type were treated as output measures and how many FTEs of each personnel type were used to produce the outputs. This is of major significance, because it means that case mix can be explicitly considered in the efficiency evaluation. That is, each case type (for example, each diagnosis-related group) can be considered as a separate output; we do not need to know the efficient relative amount of resources needed to provide care for each case type. Of course, if such efficient output-input relationships were known, more direct efficiency measures would be available, and such techniques as DEA and regression analysis would not be needed. For example, if an efficient standard cost for each type of patient care could be established, basic cost accounting techniques could be used to identify the magnitude of any inefficiencies that were present (Anthony and Reese, 1983).

Identification of the relevant outputs and inputs had to be based on an understanding of the resources that were used to provide the types of services offered in the medical-surgical area. In the study, described here, the selection of variables was also tempered by the data that would be available from the public reports issued by the hospitals.

The outputs and inputs are described in Table 1. The process of defining these outputs and inputs began with a list of all the identifiable and relevant direct outputs and inputs of the medical-surgical area. This list was refined by eliminating input measures, such as square feet of building space, which were believed to be less directly associated with efficiency and which were already reflected in part by one of the input measures used, bed days available. The panel of experts rejected physicians, housekeeping staff, nurse administration and education staff, dietary staff, and energy usage as inputs. Sherman (1981) discusses this process in detail.

The most problematic compromise in specification of outputs was the decision to use only two case types, over sixty-five years of age and

Table 1. Input and Output Data Used for DEA Evaluation of Medical-Surgical Area in Seven Teaching Hospitals

	Inputs				Outputs[a]			
Hospital	Full-Time Equivalents Nonphysician	Supply Dollars	Bed Days Available		Patient Days 65 Years of Age and Older[b]	Patient Days Under 65 Years of Age[b]	Number of Nurse Students	Number of Interns and Residents in Training
A	310.0	134,600	116,000		55,310	49,520	291	47
B	278.5	114,300	106,800		37,640	55,630	156	3
C	165.6	131,300	65,520		32,910	25,770	141	26
D	250.0	316,000	94,400		33,530	41,990	160	21
E	206.4	151,200	102,100		32,480	55,300	157	82
F	384.6	217,000	153,700		48,780	81,920	285	92
G	530.4	770,800	215,000		58,410	119,700	144	89

[a] Case mix should ideally include a more elaborate set of outputs, such as number of patient days or patients treated in each DRG category.
[b] No quality measure was available. Research was not an output of the MS area, while teaching was a distinct output of the MS area in addition to patient care.

under sixty-five years of age. DEA will ultimately be most useful when more direct and complete measures are available, such as output data on diagnosis-related groups. Such data can readily be incorporated into DEA by including each of the numerous DRG types as individual outputs, although to do so would require a considerable expansion of the sample size.

While age does appear to be a key factor in the amount of resources required to treat a patient (Bentley and Butler, 1980; Sherman, 1981), age alone is an incomplete measure. Proceeding with only age as a case mix breakdown would mean that the DEA results might be skewed because other case mix dimensions of the hospitals' outputs were not accounted for. This problem was somewhat reduced in the set of hospitals under study because they were already believed to be comparable; that is, they all treated a relatively severe (resource-intensive) set of patient diagnoses characteristic of these teaching hospitals. In addition, the medical-surgical area was moderated in the complexity of its case mix because patients were generally admitted to this area only after being stabilized in the intensive care, emergency care, or operating recovery room areas. DEA would evaluate these hospitals' use of the three inputs in Table 1 to produce patient care and training as measured by the four outputs in Table 1. To the extent that other outputs and inputs were included, the DEA results may be less than comprehensive. The experts agreed that the data specified in Table 1 were a reasonable list of the relevant outputs and inputs that characterize activities in the medical-surgical area, but they cautioned that a more detailed measure of case mix would have been a desirable addition if it had been available.

A measure of quality of care and a measure of quality of teaching are also absent because no generally accepted measure of quality was available. In any case, the experts perceived all the teaching hospitals in the study sample as providing high-quality care. The typical surrogate measures, such as mortality rates, number of malpractice law suits, and accreditation, did not suggest any obvious quality differences. Nevertheless, the absence of a quality measure means that a hospital may be inefficient because it uses additional inputs to provide a higher quality of care. This potential bias and the potential case mix bias alluded to earlier would have to be reconsidered in evaluating the DEA results.

The Results

The DEA results are summarized in Table 2, which indicates that hospitals D and G are relatively inefficient compared with the other hospitals in the data set; that is, they achieve efficiency ratings of less than one. (The names of the hospitals in the study were made available to the expert panel.)

Table 2. Results of DEA Evaluation of Medical-Surgical Areas in Seven Teaching Hospitals

Hospital	DEA Efficiency Rating	Efficiency Reference Set	Cost Per Patient Day	Cost Per Patient
A	1.0	—	$34	$408
B	1.0	—	38	418
C	1.0	—	39	429
D	0.88	A, C, E	32	407
E	1.0	—	27	343
F	1.0	—	29	348
G	0.93	E	36	324
		Average Cost	$33.57	$382.43
		Standard Deviation	$ 4.50	$ 42.51

The ratio analysis approach used by the rate-setting commission defines potentially inefficient hospitals as those with costs more than one standard deviation above the mean. There was no objective basis for this cutoff. The ratio analysis suggested that only hospital C (and specifically not hospitals D and G) might be relatively inefficient in the prices that it paid for inputs, in the amount of inputs used relative to the outputs produced, or both (columns 4 and 5 of Table 2). In fact, hospital G might be designated as the most efficient based on the cost per patient ratio. DEA goes beyond these ratios and suggests that hospitals D and G are relatively inefficient, which means that, compared to other hospitals in this group, they should be able to produce their current level of services with fewer inputs and therefore at lower cost.

Interpretation of DEA Results. The meaning of the inefficient rating derived from DEA can be understood by examining the results for hospital D. DEA indicates that hospital D is inefficient, since comparison of hospital D with all seven hospitals gives it an efficiency rating of .88. This rating means that hospital D should be able to produce its actual output level by using 12 percent—that is, $(1.00 - .88) \times 100$—less of each input than it currently does. Such efficiency gains would reduce operating costs in hospital D by more than $330,000 per year in just the medical-surgical area alone. DEA located and measured the inefficiency by comparing hospital D with its efficiency reference set—hospitals A, C, and E. The efficiency reference set (ERS) is the group of hospitals against which DEA located the inefficient hospitals and the magnitude of the inefficiency. This information is a direct output of DEA. Management of hospital D should focus on the management techniques used in hospitals A, C, and E to determine ways of reducing and improving its use of resources. This comparison is illustrated in Table 3, which indicates that a weighted composite of the efficiency reference set hospitals would yield a hypothetical hospital that produced as much in outputs or more than the inefficient hospital D but that used less in inputs than D. In this example, the composite is constructed by applying the weights (the dual variables from the DEA linear program) of 0.138, 0.296, and 0.498, respectively, to the actual outputs and inputs of hospitals A, C, and E. Columns 4, 5, and 6 of Table 3 indicate that a combination of the actual operations of these three hospitals would result in a hypothetical hospital that used 55 fewer FTEs, $182,330 fewer for supplies, and 9,090 fewer bed days to produce the same amount of patient care and thirty-four more units of training than hospital D.

Hospitals in the efficiency reference set are the relatively efficient "best practice" hospitals. This means that in the sample reported in Table 3, the DEA did not identify other hospitals that were more efficient than hospitals A, C, and E. In seeking the highest efficiency rating possible for hospital D, DEA found that it was most efficient but still inefficient compared with a composite of hospitals A, C, and E and that, if D reduced its inputs and increased its outputs by the amounts listed in column 6 of Table 3, D would be as efficient as the composite of A, C, and E. This finding represents one distinct set of operating changes that would make D efficient. Another distinct change that would make D efficient is the 12 percent reduction in all inputs noted earlier. DEA presents these and other sets of input and output adjustments that can make an inefficient unit relatively efficient. Management then has the option of selecting the operating changes that are most feasible, as I show later in this chapter. Sherman (1984) provides a detailed discussion of the interpretation of the efficiency reference set.

Experts' Assessment of DEA Results. The experts agreed that the identification of hospitals D and G as inefficient was a reasonable and believable result, although one expert expressed some doubt about the magnitude of the inefficiency found for hospital D.

The reaction of the experts provides added insights into the need for techniques like DEA. The experts were not able to rank hospitals in the study for relative efficiency before the DEA results were obtained for two reasons: First, they do not generally use output-input efficiency criteria to evaluate hospital performance; instead, they rely on such data as cost per patient and cost per day. Second, the experts were not as knowledgeable about the performance of an individual department, such as the medical-surgical area, as they were about the hospitals' overall performance. Nevertheless, their knowledge of the hospitals and of the quality of their management led them to affirm the validity of the DEA findings.

Table 3. Comparison of Hospital D with Its Efficiency Reference Set
(Hospitals A, C, and E)

	(1) Hospital A[a]		(2) Hospital C[a]		(3) Hospital E[a]		(4) Composite = (.138A + .296C + .498E)		(5) Hospital D[a]	(6) Hospital D – Composite Column (Column 5 – 4)
FTE	310		165.6		206.4		195	<	250	55
Supply Dollars	134,600		131,300		151,200		133,670	<	316,000	182,330
Bed Days	116,000		65,520		102,100		85,310	<	94,400	9,090
Nurse Training	291		141		157	=	160	=	160	—
Medicare Days	55,310	(.138)[b] +(.296)[b]	32,910	+(.498)[b]	32,480		33,530	=	33,530	—
Non-Medicare Days	49,520		25,770		55,300		41,990	=	41,990	—
Intern/Resident Training	47		26		82		55.3	>	21	-34.3

[a] Actual inputs and outputs per Table 1.
[b] Weights (dual variables) from DEA (Sherman, 1982).

Evaluation of DEA Results by Management of Hospital D. To further test the validity of the DEA results, I reviewed them with the director and the chief financial officer of inefficient hospital D. Both agreed that the medical-surgical areas of the seven hospitals were comparable and that the outputs and inputs selected for the study reasonably captured the key inputs and outputs of the area. While the case mix data were questioned, the two managers' did not feel that their case mix was more severe or resource consuming than the case mix at other hospitals in the group, so this was not believed to be the cause of the inefficiency identified in hospital D. In addition, while the managers believed that hospital D provided very high-quality care and teaching, they did not believe that the quality of care provided by their organization exceeded that of other hospitals in the group. Hence, quality was not offered as the explanation for inefficiencies located by DEA.

The director and the chief financial officer suggested three potential explanations for the inefficiencies identified by DEA. First, the supply cost data were found to be overstated by $141,000 due to an accounting transfer in the hospital's report to the rate-setting commission. This peculiarity had no effect on the data for the other six hospitals. (This suggests that DEA may be as useful as a diagnostic tool as it is as a management tool.) Second, the data on bed days were determined to be excessive. Examination of agency reports for subsequent years indicated that the figure used should be reduced by 6,935. Third, comparison of personnel levels at hospital D indicated that they were somewhat higher than levels of comparable hospitals by about 5.4 FTEs. This was a result of a conscious decision to maintain a relatively large staff so as to provide relatively personalized patient care. In summary, management of hospital D found a supply cost data problem, an excessive level of bed days available that was subsequently adjusted, and an excess FTE level that continued to exist.

The DEA evaluation was rerun with the correct supply cost data and with the reduced level of bed days to determine whether these adjustments would make hospital D efficient compared to the other six hospitals. It was found that hospital D was still inefficient compared to the other six hospitals, although its efficiency rating rose from .88 to .96 with the new data. Hence, hospital D remained inefficient, and this was believed to be due in part to personnel levels. Another DEA evaluation that reduced FTEs by the 5.4 units calculated by management in addition to the two adjustments just named was found to be adequate to make hospital D efficient compared to the other six hospitals.

As Table 4 shows, hospital D could become relatively efficient by making adjustments to its inputs that were lower in magnitude than the adjustments indicated by DEA. An inefficient hospital can select from among several different approaches in order to become relatively efficient. Alternative sets of reductions in resource use, including the one noted in

Table 4. Efficiency Adjustments Determined by DEA and Noted by Management for Hospital D

	Excessive Inputs Based on DEA Evaluation of Hospital D (Table 3)	Input Adjustments and Excesses Noted by Management of Hospital D	Cause of Excess Inputs
FTEs	55	5.4	Intentionally rich staffing
Bed Days	9,090	6,935	Elimination of 19 beds to compensate for low occupancy rate
Supply Dollars	$182,230	$141,000	Transfer due to unique accounting system

column 1 of Table 4, are available directly from DEA. Other sets of operating changes that management may consider more practical can also make a hospital relatively efficient. DEA can also be used to assess whether the particular set of operating changes proposed by management will make the hospital relatively efficient. In the case of hospital D, DEA found that the adjustments that management considered necessary (column 2 of Table 4) would indeed have the effect of making it relatively efficient.

Conclusions

The key results of this field test of DEA in a study of resource management in seven teaching hospitals in Massachusetts can be summarized as follows: First, DEA accurately identified two inefficient hospitals that the types of ratio analysis now in use were not capable of identifying. Second, DEA could explicitly consider different outputs measured in their natural units, and it was able to identify as well as to measure the relative magnitude of any inefficiency present, that is, the amount by which resource use could be reduced if these inefficient hospitals attained the operating efficiency of the relatively efficient hospitals in the study. Third, administrators familiar with the hospitals in the study could use the DEA results to help to locate the source of the inefficiency. The resulting information could lead to managerial action either to reduce the identified inefficiencies or to clarify the magnitude of the inefficiencies or slack that managers chose to incorporate into their operating plans.

Comparing DEA with Alternative Techniques. The results of the field test, taken together with the theoretical formulation and other tests of DEA described by Charnes and others, (1978, 1981) and by Sherman (1982), suggest tht DEA is a promising tool for the evaluation of hospital efficiency.

DEA has four clear advantages over the other techniques that have been used for this purpose. First, DEA is particularly useful in hospital applications, because it can simultaneously accommodate multiple outputs and inputs and because it does not require specific knowledge of the efficient absolute or relative amount of inputs required for each hospital output. Second, the hospitals labeled as inefficient are strictly inefficient, as Table 3 showed, and there is no problem of false identification of efficient hospitals as inefficient as long as all relevant outputs and inputs are included in the data set. Third, DEA indicates the general magnitude of the inefficiencies present in the inefficient hospitals. Fourth, DEA objectively locates inefficient hospitals without the need for an arbitrary cutoff point, as in ratio analysis.

DEA also has some limitations. First, DEA can only be used by comparing hospitals or hospital departments, because it locates only relatively inefficient units. Hence, it cannot locate all inefficient hospitals, because all hospitals in a given data set may be inefficient. This limitation also extends to regression techniques and to ratio analysis as used to date. Second, DEA does not identify the specific operating procedures or managerial decisions that give rise to the inefficiencies, nor does it specify the optimal path for improving efficiency. Rather, it directs the attention of managers to areas where inefficiencies exist, and it allows managers to identify changes in operating procedures that can be implemented to improve productivity.

Using DEA to Improve Hospital Technical Efficiency. The pilot study reported in this chapter suggests that DEA can be applied to hospitals in the following ways: First, the operations of segments of hospitals, such as the medical-surgical area selected for this study, as well as entire hospitals can be compared with the operations of other similar segments or hospitals in order to identify units that are relatively efficient and units that are relatively inefficient. Second, identification of relatively inefficient hospitals can be used to allocate resources so as to reduce these inefficiencies. Remedial resources can be focused on the hospitals most likely to have inefficiencies that can be reduced by in-depth study of their operations. This fact may prompt regulators or insurers to encourage, perhaps even to subsidize, the hiring of consultants or auditors to evaluate ways of increasing efficiency levels, which should ultimately lower the cost of operation, increase service levels, or both. Alternatively, it can allow regulators to direct resources to more efficient hospitals in order to encourage their growth and to help to assure that the resources that they distribute are efficiently used. Third, managers, regulators, or researchers can identify the techniques and organization designs used by more efficient hospitals. Inefficient hospitals can adopt these techniques and designs in order to improve their efficiency. As the field test suggests, DEA not only identifies the inefficient units, it also identifies the relatively efficient hospitals against which a particular hospital was found to be relatively inefficient. In this way, the number of hospitals to be compared can be significantly reduced from the number of hospitals in the group being evaluated. Fourth, regulatory organizations can use DEA to identify the more efficient hospitals as a basis for rate setting. They could require the less efficient hospitals to receive no more than the rates required to reimburse the more efficient hospitals for similar services. Such a requirement might provide an incentive for less efficient hospitals to become at least as efficient as the relatively more efficient hospitals in the data set. DEA can also be used with multiperiod data to assess whether new reimbursement techniques and other incentives result in increased efficiency. Such a use of DEA would indicate whether hospitals or hospital departments were becoming more or less efficient compared with themselves and with other hospitals over time.

DEA has capabilities not found in other measurement techniques, such as ratio analysis. At the same time, other techniques can address efficiency dimensions that DEA does not address. For example, purchasing such inputs as personnel and drugs at the lowest price, a practice often referred to as *price efficiency,* is not addressed with DEA. Price efficiency can, however, be reasonably analyzed by comparing ratios of cost per FTE, cost per unit of a drug, and so forth. Moreover, other analytic techniques are needed to locate the specific cause of inefficiencies identified by DEA. Thus, DEA is a useful complement to, not a replacement for, other analytic techniques that have been used to improve hospital management.

The results of this study and the positive response to applications of DEA in other organizational settings provide strong evidence that DEA may well be effective in improving resource utilization in acute care hospitals, preferred provider organizations, health maintenance organizations, and rehabilitation hospitals. DEA's potential in helping to rationalize the establishment of common reimbursement rates that reflect a relatively efficient level of service is as yet untested, but it may prove to be highly beneficial, and it certainly warrants serious research as evidence of DEA's capabilities continues to accumulate.

References

Anthony, R. N., and Reese, J. S. *Accounting: Text and Cases.* Homewood, Ill.: Irwin, 1983.

Bentley, J. D., and Butler, P. W. *Describing and Paying Hospitals: Developments in Patient Case Mix.* Washington, D.C.: Association of American Medical Colleges, 1980.

Biles, B., Schramm, C. J., and Atkinson, J. G. "Hospital Cost Inflation Under State Rate-Setting Programs." *New England Journal of Medicine,* 1980, *303,* 664-668.

Bowlin, W. F., Charnes, A., Cooper, W. W., and Sherman, H. D. "Data Envelopment Analysis and Regression Approaches to Efficiency Estimation and Evaluation." *Annuals of Operation Research,* 1985, *2,* 113-138.

Charnes, A., Cooper, W. W., and Rhodes, E. "Measuring the Efficiency of Decision-Making Units." *European Journal of Operational Research,* 1978, *2* (6), 429-444.

Charnes, A., Cooper, W. W., and Rhodes, E. "Evaluating Program and Managerial Efficiency: An Application of Data Envelopment Analysis to Program Follow Through." *Management Science,* 1981, 27 (6), 668-697.

Feldstein, M. *Economic Analysis for Health Service Efficiency.* Amsterdam: North-Holland, 1968.

Forsund, F. R., Knox-Lovell, C. A., and Schmidt, P. "A Survey of Frontier Production Functions and of Their Relationship to Efficiency Measurement." *Journal of Econometrics,* 1980, *13,* 5-25.

General Accounting Office. *Rising Hospital Costs Can Be Restrained by Regulating Payment and Improving Management.* Washington, D.C.: General Accounting Office, 1980.

Hospital Bureau, Massachusetts Rate Setting Commission. *Grouping of Hospitals for Purposes of Determining Reasonable Cost Levels.* Document No. 114.1 CMR. Boston: Massachusetts Rate Setting Commission, 1980.

Massachusetts Rate Setting Commission. *Commonwealth of Massachusetts Hospitals Uniform Reporting Manual.* Boston, Massachusetts Rate Setting Commission, 1978.

Massachusetts Rate Setting Commission. "Executive Summary: FY 1981 Groups of Hospitals." Unpublished document. Boston: Massachusetts Rate Setting Commission, 1980.

Sherman, H. D. "Measurement of Hospital Technical Efficiency: A Comparative Evaluation of Data Envelopment Analysis and Other Efficiency Measurement Techniques for Measuring and Locating Inefficiency in Health Care Organizations." Unpublished doctoral dissertation. Graduate School of Business Administration, Harvard University, 1981.

Sherman, H. D. *Identifying Inefficiencies in Multiple Output-Multiple Input Organizations.* Working Paper #1316-82. Cambridge, Mass.: Sloan School of Management, Massachusetts Institute of Technology, 1982.

Sherman, H. D. "Data Envelopment Analysis as a New Managerial Audit Methodology—Test and Evaluation." *Auditing—A Journal of Practice and Theory,* 1984, *4* (2), 35-53.

H. David Sherman is associate professor in the College of Business Administration at Northeastern University, Boston, Massachusetts.

Data envelopment analysis and related techniques are applied in an evaluation of the performance efficiency of various classifications of national parks.

An Exploratory Analysis of Variations in Performance Among U.S. National Parks

Eduardo L. Rhodes

The establishment of Yellowstone National Park by Congress in March 1872 "as a public park or pleasuring ground for the benefit and enjoyment of the people" signaled the beginnings of a national commitment and focus on the preservation and study of natural and historical resources. This commitment received its greatest impetus with the creation by Congress in 1916 of the National Park Service (NPS) within the U.S. Department of Interior. In the years since the NPS was established, its mission has expanded to include oversight of much more than just the large-acreage national parks and monuments, such as Yellowstone and Yosemite. Since the 1930s, NPS has assumed primary responsibility for many of the nationally significant historical and military sites of the country, such as

---

The majority of the work described in this chapter was performed in 1980 and 1981 while the author was a Brookings Institution Economic Policy Fellow assigned to the Office of Policy Analysis, U.S. Department of the Interior, Washington, D.C. The author wishes to thank the staff of the Policy Analysis office and numerous office personnel from the National Park Service who provided crucial data, reviewed study conceptualizations, and generally put up with an at times naive academician.

Gettysburg National Military Park, Harpers Ferry National Historical Park, and Abraham Lincoln Birthplace National Historic Site. At the present time, the National Park Service is responsible for a park system of over 320 geographically dispersed units that cover nearly 100 million acres of land and attract millions of visitors every year.

Additions to the system and classification of specific lands or sites are by Congressional action, with NPS and Interior providing advisement. For this reason and others, the Park Service finds itself managing a vast empire whose constituents have seemingly very different needs and goals and whose importance to the natural resource and historic heritage of this country is quite varied.

Today, in both the public and the Department of Interior, there is a growing awareness of the urgent management challenges that face the parks (General Accounting Office, 1980; National Park Service, 1981). These challenges, such as severe restrictions on funding for capital improvements, increasing environmental threats from without the park system, deteriorating facilities, and paradoxically concurrent expansion of the scope of park responsibilities, place a high premium on improvements in the management of park operations. Unfortunately, the Park Service, a very tradition-bound organization, has been slow to recognize the validity of comparing the overall performance of different parks. In fact, most past studies of national parks have tended to focus on only one or two dimensions of an individual park's activities or responsibilities.

These past studies examining park performance can be divided into two broad categories. The category that treats aspects of the biological and environmental preservation and management mission of the Park Service is the larger of the two. The studies in this category investigate such issues as the effect of increases in use of backcountry trails on the well-being of certain park flora and fauna (Liddle, 1975; Schmidly and Ditton, 1978; Shelby, 1980; Stankey, 1973; Wildland Research Center, 1962) or the danger posed to park wildlife by external disturbances, such as nearby industrial development, mineral exploration, or geothermal drilling (National Park Service, 1981). The second category of park studies examines narrowly defined maintenance or management issues, such as deterioration in park physical facilities and support systems (General Accounting Office, 1980), the rise in park vandalism, and the desirability of introducing multiple-part pricing into the park usage fee structure (Cicchetti and others, 1973; Penz, 1975).

All the studies just mentioned leave questions about how well the parks use the resources that have been provided largely unanswered. That is, Park Service decision makers have not been able or willing to compare the performance of one park operation with the performance of any other park operation except on some very narrowly defined dimensions (Fisher and Krutilla, 1972; Lee, 1975; Stankey, 1972, 1973; Wise and Cole, 1978). The few management studies that do exist focus on the application of a new procedure or technique, such as computer simulation or control theory, to a subset of a park's mission responsibilities, usually some aspect of the recreational management and provision question.

It should also be noted that most of the studies just mentioned were park specific, involving no more than two or at most three parks. This individual focus is consistent with an attitude, shared by many within the Park Service, that each park is unique and that each park has a different set of operating and environmental conditions and problems. This uniqueness, it is argued, invalidates any performance comparisons across parks. Such an attitude stems in part from past difficulties both in defining the mission of the Park Service and in evaluating the individual parts of that mission.

In the late 1970s, the Office of Policy Analysis under the U.S. Secretary of Interior became interested in analyzing the general operations of parks. Developing a general approach to evaluation of the park mission was one of my major responsibilities during a fifteen-month appointment to the Office of Policy Analysis as a Brookings Institution Economic Policy Fellow in 1980 and 1981. The office believed that the investment of a considerable amount of front-end time in cultivating the trust and eliciting the cooperation of key Park Service personnel would make it possible to conduct a reasonably valid mission or performance study. Furthermore, the office believed that certain evaluation tools provided by management science could overcome some of the technical problems encountered in past attempts to appraise park performance. Data envelopment analysis (DEA) was the tool chosen for this study. As developed by Charnes and others (1978, 1981) and by Rhodes (1978), DEA calculates a nonlinear ratio definition of output to input efficiency that is quite similar to the efficiency definition found in the physical sciences and in engineering.

Three of DEA's features were especially attractive for the evaluation of park performance. First, it could treat multiple output-input processes, of which park operations are classic examples. Second, without making some of the more restrictive assumptions of traditional production analysis, which in the case of the national parks would be hard if not impossible to justify, DEA estimates a scalar measure of the performance efficiency for individual units. Third, as Banker (1980, forthcoming) and Banker and others (1984) have shown, the DEA efficiency value can be separated into a technical and a scale efficiency component that provide some insight into the relation between park size and efficiency, although the use of the methodology for this purpose will not be discussed in this chapter.

On a general level, the problems encountered in this study of park performance are representative of the whole area of natural resource management in the public sector. This area suffers more than others, such as education and health care, from measurement problems and from the absence of a firm analytic tradition on which much of public policy analysis depends. Thus, the park study can be viewed as an initial attempt to address some of these general natural resource management issues.

The Park Study Project

This chapter reports on my first efforts to deal with the problems inherent in a comprehensive performance evaluation of parks. These efforts included the formulation of a series of general park mission models and, as noted earlier, an application of data envelopment analysis to the evaluation of some dimensions of efficiency in park performance.

The formulation of park mission models systematically varied input and output elements. Such variation was necessary at this early stage of investigation for three reasons: First, current measurement capabilities make it difficult to portray the natural resource management activity process precisely. In a number of cases, the model variations were simply different versions of the same underlying phenomenon. For example, to measure visitor contact by park agents, the number of visitor contacts is used in one model, while the number of conducted trips in which contacts are made is used in another. It should be noted that, for the reason of measurement reliability, no conclusive policy recommendations were put forth in the study summary. Second, even assuming a substantial improvement in our ability to measure quality and quantity, there was substantial conflict over park missions. Within the Park Service itself, there was little consensus on what a park's total mission responsibilities were. Needless to say, there was even less agreement on the relative importance of any particular element or dimension of that mission. Third, regardless of stated preferences or goals, certain activities or services—for example, increasing visitation counts—often seemed to receive special attention, based upon a belief that these activities were what "really" determined a park's funding and appraisal by Washington.

The model variations were conducted in two general directions: first, in order to favor one park mission over another (for example, historic preservation over natural preservation or visitor services); second, in order to favor number of services provided over number of those affected by the services (for example, number of visitor contacts during a guided trip over number of guided trips provided).

The second major phase of the study reported in this chapter submitted the estimation results of a "representative" model specification to rigorous examination. Together, these steps laid the groundwork for an exploratory investigation of several policy questions. The policy questions chosen were based on what numerous Park Service officials and other members of Interior viewed as possible imbalances in the resource allocation and park management systems. Four questions were asked: First, do certain parks overemphasize visitation and as a result neglect other park mission goals? Second, given the "informal" supervisory status determination system now current in the Park Service, is there a tendency in the larger or more politically powerful parks toward above-normal buildup of manpower levels? Third, in view of the fact that the way in which a particular park is classified (for example, as a National Park) is based on the perceived significance of its total mission, has resource allocation among parks oversupported certain classifications of parks relative to their actual performance? Fourth, in spite of supposedly general mission objectives, is there a difference in performance or efficiency between natural resources parks and the so-called historic parks possibly as a result of the more senior status of the natural resource–preserving parks?

The Park Model. In seeking a suitable conceptual framework upon which to construct park models, it is tempting to adopt the classical production function concept and approach of economics. Under this concept, one makes an analogy between the activities of a park and the production activities of a firm in the private sector. It follows from the analog that park management provides or produces a collection of public and private goods and services by manipulating a collection of activities or resource inputs, such as park manpower, facilities, and equipment.

One problem posed by the economic model is that it requires us to specify not only the content but also the underlying form of the production function. When the production function has multiple outputs, as it does in the case of the parks, the economic model approach becomes even more problematic. To summarize, then, the considerable variation in park types, location, and resource mix made it highly unlikely that a single common model could successfully depict all parks. Moreover, the information and relationship specification necessary to complete a multiple output depiction of park activities within the traditional economic framework was clearly beyond the level of current natural resource management analysis capabilities. In any case, the absence of convenient cost and price measurements precluded use of the budgetary ratio approach favored in economics.

In contrast, data envelopment analysis handles all the difficulties just mentioned. DEA permits unspecified production functions to differ from one park to another. In fact, as long as there is agreement across parks about the nature of the inputs and outputs used, we can evaluate the relative efficiency of each park unit even if each of the approximately 320 NPS park units operates with a unique function. In addition, DEA permits the treatment of multiple output activities with only minimum specification of relationships among model elements.

Major Mission Functions. For the reasons just outlined, I decided to use the power of DEA for my analysis of mission performance of national parks. Variable identification and data generation were the result of a joint effort involving a number of policy and information units of the NPS and the Office of Policy Analysis group in the Department of Interior. Using data collected from the NPS Washington, D.C. office and its

Denver Service Center, and DEA procedures, I evaluated the mission performance of eighty parks that represented a variety of mission orientations.

After spending seven months interviewing Interior personnel, both inside and outside the Park Service, I was sure about one thing: Beyond a very general notion of responsibility for the management of natural or historic resources, there was little agreement or thought about the total mission of a given park. Internal NPS management policies guidelines (National Park Service, 1979a) cite several responsibilities based on legislated service mandates. At the same time, these guidelines stress the need for each park to develop a general management plan that includes a statement of the park's purpose and its management objectives. While this emphasis is consistent with the notion that each park is unique, a philosophy held by some in the Service, the resulting park-specific management plans were almost totally useless as a basis for systemwide evaluation. Furthermore, at the time when I conducted my study, only a handful of parks had developed such a plan.

However, by relying primarily on information supplied by policy, budget, and Park Service operations groups, I identified four major mission categories, which my respondents agreed were common to almost all park operations: The natural preservation and resource protection function involves the preservation, restoration, and management of natural resources, including land, waterways, natural phenomena, and native flora and fauna (National Park Service, 1979a). The historic and cultural preservation and resource protection function addresses the management and preservation of cultural, historic, and prehistoric sites, structures, and artifacts and conducts research on these resources (National Park Service, 1979a; Cultural Resource Division, National Park Service, 1980). The interpretive and visitor services function concerns educational services or activities provided for visitors by park rangers, naturalists, historians, archeologists, and interpretive technicians (National Park Service, 1979a). The visitor protection function involves the assisting and protecting of visitors involved in recreational use and esthetic enjoyment of the park (National Park Service, 1979a). In addition, two supporting functions were identified. The facilities and maintenance function includes such activities as road building, structure maintenance, and repair, and the support and administrative services function includes the administrative services that support all activities related to the four mission goals.

After specifying the general mission or outputs of a park operation, it became necessary to consider the measurement of these outputs. The resources or inputs used to achieve those outputs also needed to be measured. Unfortunately, especially for the outputs, direct measurement is extremely difficult if not impossible. Such information has generally not been collected due either to funding constraints or to the absence of valid measures. As a result of these measurement problems, my study used surrogate variables that depicted critical dimensions of the actual outputs and inputs. We were reasonably successful in this endeavor except for the two support categories, facilities maintenance and support/administrative services. However, to the degree that the outputs of these mission functions are contained in the surrogates used for other outputs, they are represented, albeit imperfectly, in the models chosen.

The Surrogate Output Variables. This section groups each set of surrogate variables by the mission goals that the variables describe. A brief explanation of the reason for the choice is added where needed, and the major shortcoming of each surrogate is described. The preservation of natural resources function has a single surrogate variable, ACRES. ACRES is a measure of the total acreage that a park operation is responsible for maintaining. It would have been advantageous to refine this measurement by distinguishing between natural zone acreage and historic zone acreage. That is, using the Park Service's own classification system, we would measure only those areas within a given park for which preservation responsibilities were valid. Unfortunately, these zone designations are part of the park management plan that few parks had completed at the time of my study. The ACRES measure also suffers from the absence of a quality dimension. That is, it does not measure variances in the quality of preservation that park managers achieve on their acres. Such a measurement does not exist. The closest equivalent involves an NPS attempt to take a census of park flora and fauna. However, this measurement was not available at the time of my study.

There are a number of variables related to the preservation of historic/cultural resources mission:

- HIST BLDG: Number of classified buildings in park (a classified building, structure, or site is one that has been placed on the National Register of Historic Places).
- HIST ENG: Number of classified engineering structures
- TOT HIST: Total number of classified structures; includes as subsets HIST BLDG (buildings), HIST ENG (engineering structures), and several other categories of classified structures
- PREHIST: Number of prehistoric structures in park
- MUS CAT: Number of catalogued museum artifacts
- MUS TOT: Total number of artifacts in museum collection, has MUS CAT as a subset.

As in the case of the ACRES measure, there is no measure of the quality of historic/cultural preservation achieved with each item.

The visitor interpretive and recreational services function and the visitor protection function present some problems. Because it is impractical to test visitors before and after their park experience in order to measure the degree to which their visit has improved their understanding of the environment or their appreciation for the importance of preservation, we have used measures of visitor contacts with various park education programs. Visitor protection is so entwined with visitor recreational services that it was difficult to find surrogates that measured them separately. Thus, the surrogate variables listed here depict aspects of the personal service educational goal, the more self-directed interpretive services, and recreational services that include visitor protection:

- TRIP NUM: Number of conducted educational trips
- TRIP VIS: Number of visitor contacts via conducted educational trips
- TALKS NUM: Number of live talk contacts
- TALK VIS: Number of visitor contacts via live talks
- TRAIL VIS: Number of people using trails
- VIS CENT: Number of visitors using visitor center (in most parks, the visitor center is considered the focal point for recreational and educational park-directed activities)
- VIS REC: Total number of recreational visits to park
- VIS HRS: Total number of recreation hours spent in park
- P-CAMP: Number of overnight stays at park-run campsites
- P-BACK: Number of overnight camping stays in backcountry.

Park Management Inputs. Land can be viewed as an input into the visitor services activities of a park. Under ideal conditions, the portion of land devoted to such activities would be included as an input. In contrast, the land on which only preservation activities were conducted would be excluded as an input. In the ideal situation, all interdependency and interaction effects among land uses would be accounted for, along with interdependencies among outputs. Unfortunately, such an ideal is presently unattainable, because neither the measurement tools nor the data needed for making such distinctions is available. Thus, I collected information on NPS activities or resource commitments that included dimensions of the land as a recreation or education input. For example, miles of roads and trails were treated as capital variables. The mixed characteristics of some input variables were recognized by labeling them *capital-land* measurements. Note that capital is defined as an input produced in some earlier period of production, for example, buildings, roads, trails, and maintenance equipment.

There were three manpower or labor input variables:

- EMP PERM: Permanent full-time employees listed by total months of employment
- EMP LIM: Less than full-time career employees listed by total number of months worked (this category includes many of the permanent employees who are released by parks during the winter shutdown or off-season periods)
- EMP TEMP: Temporary employees listed by total months worked (these are primarily summertime workers).

Principal park manpower has been separated into these three categories in order to capture some of the variation in labor quality.

Six variables were chosen to represent the capital/land input:
- VIS BLG: Number of visitor-oriented buildings
- VIS AREA: Square feet of visitor-oriented building space
- NVIS BLG: Number of non-visitor-oriented buildings, for example, maintenance buildings, workshops, and administrative structures
- NVIS AREA: Square feet of non-visitor-oriented building space
- TRAILS: Miles of trails
- ROADS: Miles of roads.

Table 1 summarizes all the measurement elements chosen along with their associated mission goals or input categories.

The Parks

While all National Park Service units that follow the four mission functions listed earlier are generally termed *parks* within the service, only the members of a subset are called *national parks*. There are nearly two dozen different park classifications (National Park Service, 1979b). These official classifications, which are legislated by Congress, represent the political importance of each park's sponsor as much as they represent a park's mission responsibilities.

For the purposes of comparing performance, we must classify parks in terms of managerially important categories. While numerous valid clustering arrangements could be made, the grouping scheme that I chose used principal functional responsibilities and scale of operation to separate the NPS units. My scheme had six classifications:

- *Large land-preserving units* (30,000 acres or more). The apparent predominant objective of these parks is the preservation and protection of natural resources, such as land and waterways; natural phenomena, such as geysers; and all associated native flora and fauna. Examples: Zion National Park, Death Valley National Park, Yosemite National Park
- *Other land-preserving units* (at least 2,000 acres but less than 30,000 acres). Examples: Lehman Caves National Monument, Virgin Islands National Park, Wind Cave National Park
- *Large historic-preserving units* (more than 1,000 acres of land). These parks focus on historic or cultural preservation. Examples: Saratoga National Historical Park, Custer Battlefield National Monument, Gettysburg National Military Park, Ninety-Six National Historic Site
- *Other historic-preserving units* (less than 1,000 acres of land). Examples: John Muir National Historic Site, Fort McHenry

Table 1. Summary of Mission Goals and Input Categories

Park Mission Goals or Outputs	Measurement Variables
Preservation of Natural Resources	ACRES
Preservation of Historical/Cultural Resources	HIST BLDG
	HIST ENG
	TOT HIST
	PREHIST
	MUS CAT
	MUS TOT
Visitor Interpretive and Recreational Services plus Visitor Protection	TRIP NUM
	TRIP VIS
	TALK NUM
	TALK VIS
	TRAIL VIS
	VIS CENT
	VIS REC
	VIS HRS
	C-LODGE
	P-CAMP
	P-BACK
Park Operations Inputs	
Manpower Resources	EMP PERM
	EMP LIM
	EMP TEMP
	YCC
	YACC
Capital/Land Resources	VIS BLG
	VIS AREA
	NVIS BLG
	NVIS AREA
	TRAILS
	ROADS

National Monument and Historic Shrine, Sitka National Historic Park

- *National Recreation Areas.* These parks, which are usually about equal in size to the large land-preserving parks, tend to emphasize recreational services and experiences over preservation or reclamation. Examples: Gateway National Recreation Area, Glen Canyon National Recreation Area, Lake Mead National Recreation Area
- *Special units.* These parks truly are unique and defy categorization into any of the above classifications. Examples: Blue Ridge Parkway, National Mall (Washington, D.C.), Wolf Trap Park for the Performing Arts.

Of the six mission groups, only three were included in my study: large land-preserving units, large historic-preserving units, and National Recreation Areas. Data-gathering capabilities and limits on time precluded use of the other three park groups. Two categories—other land-preserving units and other historic-preserving units—were similar enough to their larger counterparts that the overall utility of the study should not be diminished by their absence. The last mission category, the catch-all special units group, was incommensurable with the scope of the study. That is, each of these special units was so unique that comparisons with other units were not easy to justify. For example, the Blue Ridge Parkway is essentially the highway that traverses the crest of the Blue Ridge Mountains, while the National Mall is the park area that extends from the Capitol Building to the Washington Monument.

To calculate park efficiency, five DEA runs were conducted over eighty park units. Sixty-five parks were either large land-preserving units or National Recreation Areas. The remaining fifteen parks were large historic preserving units. The aim of these runs was to detect general patterns in park operating efficiency. By changing the input-output mix, we increased or decreased the chances that parks with slightly different areas of mission emphasis would be rated efficient.

In DEA efficiency calculations, the chances that a unit has of being good enough in terms of at least one input or output increase as the mix of inputs and outputs increases. Thus, varying both the number and the composition of input-output mixes means that the input or output factor in which a given unit is strong has the effect either of making that factor predominate or, conversely, of eliminating it, and the unit's efficiency rating increases or decreases as a result.

The five DEA models are presented in Table 2. The runs are classified in terms of mission emphasis or variable mix. Run 1 was a general mission run with a representative input-output mix. Run 2 emphasized the purely recreational over more strenuous backcountry and trail activities. Thus, trail and road inputs were excluded, as were all camping and backpacking-related outputs. Note that the historic attributes of the parks were included. Run 3 examined efficiency conditions when the visitation/employees criterion was the primary output determinant. Thus, only numbers of different classes of employees were used as inputs, and number of recreational visits and acres of land were used as outputs. Run 4 placed the emphasis on historic parks. Trail and road input variables were not included, and overnight stays of any kind were excluded as output variables. All historic inputs, such as classified structures, museum collections, and prehistoric structures, were included, as were the number and size measures of conducted tours and live talks, both of which the historically oriented parks tend to emphasize. Run 5 resembled run 3 with another mix of inputs and outputs which resulted in a narrower definition of park operations and mission. This run included those factors most commonly associated with national parks.

Table 2. Efficiency Run Inputs and Outputs

INPUTS	Run #1	#2	#3	#4	#5
Number of Permanent Employees	X	X	X	X	X
Number of Less-Than-Full-Time Employees	X	X	X	X	X
Number of Temporary Employees	X	X	X	X	
Area of Visitor-Oriented Buildings	X				X
Number of Non-Visitor-Oriented Buildings		X		X	
Area of Non-Visitor-Oriented Buildings	X			X	X
Miles of Trail	X			X	X
Miles of Road	X				X
OUTPUTS					
Number of Conducted Trips		Y		Y	
Number of Trip Visitor Contacts	Y			Y	Y
Number of Live Talks		Y		Y	
Number of Live Talk Contacts	Y			Y	Y
Number of People on Trails	Y				
Number of Classified Buildings	Y				Y
Total Classified Structures		Y			
Visitor Center Contacts	Y	Y		Y	Y
Number of Recreational Visits		Y	Y	Y	
Number of Recreational Visitor Hours	Y				Y
Number of Overnight Stays at Campsites	Y				
Number of Overnight Stays in Backcountry	Y				
Number of Catalogued Museum Artifacts				Y	
Total Number of Artifacts in Park Collection	Y	Y			
Number of Prehistoric Structures	Y	Y		Y	
Acres	Y	Y	Y	Y	Y

Note: X or Y indicates that the variable was included in the run.

Results

Table 3 identifies the parks in each run that had an efficiency score of one by means of an asterisk. Given the rudimentary level of measurement instruments in this study area, the results should be viewed as very exploratory and tentative. In this section, we will examine the results of several runs that highlight some interesting production hypotheses or operations characteristics.

One of the most heated discussions within park management circles centers on whether some parks follow too narrow a recreation orientation as a result of which they beef up their visitation numbers at the expense of their responsibilities for the management of natural resources. The results of run 3 challenge such a line of argument. This model specified a very narrow definition of the park objective function, as comparisons were made only on the basis of manpower usage and park visitation. As Table 3 reveals, fifty-nine of the sixty-five large land-preserving parks or National Recreation Areas and fourteen of the fifteen historic-preserving parks were evaluated as inefficient in run 3; that is, they had efficiency value of less than one. The implication is that, if we restrict the guiding performance criterion to visitor/employee ratios, as some have argued that we should, few parks are performing efficiently. However, a more realistic interpretation of the results of run 3 is that other responsibilities besides simple visitation are receiving operation attention and resource allocation. (Note, however, that, as the set of inputs and outputs decreases, the nature of the DEA calculation method causes generally fewer units to receive high efficiency ratings.)

Close inspection of the few parks in run 3 that received efficiency scores of one prompt other questions. For example, these parks have very high visitor/manpower ratios. But, given the absence from our model of a measure of quality of visitation or amount of service, these efficient parks may in fact be grossly understaffed, and thus they may be providing rather poor service. All things being equal, run 3 favors parks with small staffs that offer few services and parks that receive many short visitations during daylight hours. For example, the Golden Gate National Recreation Area, which had an efficiency score of one on run 3, is a highly visited urban recreation area that has no overnight or camping accommodations; visitors tend to stay less than half the day. Thus, from a management perspective, run 3 provides little evidence to support the suspicion that a large number of parks are exclusively following a simple visitation performance goal criterion. Of course, it is quite possible that some parks place an extraordinary emphasis on visitation, but, since they pay some attention to other objectives, they are not identified in run 3 as pursuing this narrow objective.

Run 4 is interesting for its historical orientation. Given the absence of certain recreational outputs, such as the camping variables, we would

Table 3. Efficiency Status on Multiple Runs

Large Land-Preserving Units
(Acres > 30,000)

Study #	Park Name	Run #				
1	Badlands NP	*	*	*	*	*
2	Bryce Canyon NP					
3	Canyonlands NP	*			*	*
4	Capital Reef NP	*	*		*	*
5	Dinosaur NM					*
6	Glacier NP	*				*
7	Grand Teton NP					
8	Great Sand Dunes NM					
9	Mesa Verde NP	*	*		*	*
10	Rocky Mountain NP	*	*		*	*
11	Theodore Roosevelt NP					
12	Yellowstone NP	*			*	*
13	Zion NP					
14	Acadia NP	*	*		*	*
15	Cape Cod NS	*			*	*
16	Prince Williams Forest NP	*	*	*	*	*
17	Assateague Island NS	*				*
18	Shenandoah NP					
19	Biscayne NP	*				*
20	Canaveral NS				*	
21	Cape Hatteras NS	*				
22	Cumberland Island NS				*	
23	Everglades NP	*				
24	Fort Jefferson NM	*			*	
25	Great Smoky Mountains NP	*			*	
26	Gulf Island NS	*				
27	Mammoth Cave NP				*	
28	Apostle Islands NL	*				

Table 3. *(continued)*

Large Land-Preserving Units
(Acres > 30,000)

Study #	Park Name		Run #			
29	Isle Royal NP	*				*
30	Pictured Rocks NL	*				
31	Sleeping Bear Dunes NL	*			*	
32	Voyageurs NP	*				*
33	Bandelier NM	*				
34	Big Bend NP	*	*		*	
35	Canyon de Cehlly NM	*	*		*	*
36	Carlsbad Caverns NP	*	*		*	*
37	Guadalupe Mountains NP	*			*	
38	Wupatki NM	*				
39	Death Valley NP	*	*		*	*
40	Grand Canyon NP	*				
41	Hawaii Volcanoes NP	*	*		*	*
42	Joshua Tree NM	*	*		*	*
43	Lassen Volcanic NP					
44	Lava Beds NM					
45	Organ Pipe Cactus NM	*	*		*	
46	Petrified Forest NP	*	*		*	*
47	Point Reyes NS		*		*	
48	Redwood NP					
49	Saguaro NM	*	*	*	*	
50	Sequoia NP					
51	Yosemite NP	*				
52	Crater Lake NP	*				
53	Craters of the Moon NM					
54	Mt. McKinley NP	*	*	*	*	*
55	North Cascades NP					

Table 3. *(continued)*

National Recreation Areas
(Acres > 30,000)

56	Bighorn Canyon NRA					
57	Curecanti NRA	*				
58	Glen Canyon NRA	*	*		*	
59	Delaware Water Gap NRA	*				
60	Cuyahoga Valley NRA	*			*	
61	Lake Meredith NRA	*			*	
62	Golden Gate NRA	*	*	*	*	*
63	Lake Mead NRA	*			*	*
64	Whiskeytown-Shasta-Trinity NRA					
65	Coulee Dam NRA	*	*			

Acres > 1,000

66	Antietam NB	*	*		*	*
67	Chaco Canyon NM	*	*		*	*
68	Chickamauga and Chattanooga NMP	*	*		*	*
69	Colonial NHP	*	*	*		
70	Fredericksburg and Spottsylvania County Battlefield NMP		*		*	
71	Gettysburg NMP	*	*		*	*
72	Golden Spike NHS	*	*		*	*
73	Horseshoe Bend NMP					
74	Kennesaw Mountain NMP	*	*	*	*	*
75	Kings Mountain NMP					
76	Manassas NBP	*	*		*	*
77	Nez Perce NMP					
78	Saratoga NMP					
79	Shiloh NMP					
80	Valley Forge NHP	*	*		*	*

Note: NB = National Battleﬁeld
NBP = National Battleﬁeld Park
NHP = National Historic Park
NHS = National Historic Site
NL = National Lakeshore
NM = National Monument
NMP = National Military Park
NP = National Park
NRA = National Recreation Area
NS = National Seashore

expect the historical parks to achieve a better rating on this run than their land-preserving or recreation counterparts do. And, indeed, we find that the historic-preserving parks performed well on run 4. Of fifteen historic-preserving parks, ten—more than 66 percent—had an efficiency score of one. In contrast, when the sixty-five large land-preserving parks and National Recreation Areas were evaluated under the same operational definition, fewer than 50 percent had an efficiency score of one. It does appear, then, that the historic-preserving parks are engaged in a different production activity from that pursued by other parks. In contrast, in run 1, which was more inclusive, better than 70 percent of the large parks were evaluated as efficient, while 60 percent of the historic-preserving parks were evaluated as efficient—almost as many as in run 4.

Special attention might be paid to the parks that were found to be efficient under all the input-output specifications and to the parks that were found to be inefficient under all specifications. Only five parks received efficiency scores of one for all runs. Conversely, thirteen received efficiency scores of less than one for all runs. These cases raise two questions. First, is there any similarity among the parks with all ones? Second, what accounts for the fact that certain parks are never efficient, that is, that these parks never locate on the efficiency frontier?

It is obvious that an efficiency problem exists for the parks with consistently low efficiency scores. However, review of the results of all five runs reveals no specific patterns of weakness. The course of action under such circumstances that is consistent with DEA's role as the first step in a management investigation is to inspect the operating history of these parks. For example, Redwood National Park is relatively new. Because of its newness and because of the agency's method of manpower allocation, visitation at Redwood may not yet have built up to the levels anticipated by the current permanent staffing. One way of testing this hypothesis is by conducting a time-oriented DEA calculation; that is, Redwood's production efficiency should be analyzed in a multiyear framework. In such an analysis, we would expect to find the efficiency scores for Redwood National Park becoming progressively higher over time if newness is the reason for its current performance.

We can also employ the same individual case approach to the five parks that consistently receive efficiency scores of one. It may be that we do not have five examples of great operation performance but rather five examples of understaffed and/or underequipped parks. If that is indeed the case, it provides an excellent example of how inspection of the supposedly "good" extremes can reveal just as serious an operations problem as inspection of the lowest-rated parks. This conclusion is reinforced by the fact that manipulation of input-output combinations gave all parks an opportunity to stand out in their identified areas of program emphasis. However, it is extremely unlikely that a park would retain its perfect efficiency score under all operation definitions. Indeed, it could be argued that vigorous pursuit of one objective can be accomplished only at the expense of lowered performance in some other area. For a park to be at the top of the scale in both areas suggests problems of quality or effectiveness.

A General Run Analysis

To demonstrate the utility of DEA, we will now focus on the results of run 1. This general mission run contains inputs and outputs that represent almost all the various park missions: Both land-preserving and recreational and educational mission elements are included. Table 4 displays the efficiency values estimated for each of the eighty park units in the sample.

Inspecting these results, we note that fifty-four park units—nearly two-thirds of the set—have the maximum efficiency value of one. Looking at the units with an efficiency value of less than one, we observe a rather wide dispersion, which is depicted in Figure 1. These twenty-six values range from .266 to .987.

The interpretation of these DEA efficiency results in light of the policy questions raised earlier has particular interest at this point in the discussion. In order to accomplish this aim, we perform a series of comparative parametric and nonparametric tests and examinations of the DEA results along several different classification systems. Note that less powerful nonparametric tests are included here to avoid questions about the propriety of relying solely on parametric testing on the DEA value differences.

Our first series of comparisons is by type of park. The tests in this series compare large land-preserving units and National Recreation Areas with historic-preserving units. Another series of comparisons centers on the land-preserving units and the National Recreation Areas. The tests in this series compare the national parks with land-preserving units that have other designations, such as *national monument, national lakeshore,* and *National Recreation Area.* The last series of tests compares the National Recreation Areas (which, as noted earlier, also have a land-preserving mission) with the land-preserving units. During my interviews with Interior personnel, some suggested that NRAs place slightly less emphasis on their preservation responsibilities. If they do, it may in some cases show up as a loss in overall performance efficiency.

The importance of the first series of sample comparisons lies in detecting any broad type-specific political or popularity bias in resource allocation that results in lower performance efficiency. To state the issue of interest as a question, would excess or relatively unwarranted input usage cause "favored" parks to perform below parks of other types? Table 5 summarizes the results of these comparisons.

Table 4. Efficiency Values in Run 1

#	Park Name	DEA Value (h_0)	#	Park Name	DEA Value (h_0)	#	Park Name	DEA Value (h_0)	#	Park Name	DEA Value (h_0)
Classification #1:			23	Everglades NP	1.000	45	Organ Pipe Cactus NM	1.000	64	Whiskeytown-Shasta-Trinity NRA	.640
Large Land-Preserving Units			24	Fort Jefferson NM	1.000	46	Petrified Forest NP	1.000	65	Coulee Dam NRA	1.000
1	Badlands NP	1.000	25	Great Smokey Mountains NP	1.000	47	Point Reyes NS	.616	*Classification #3*		
2	Bryce Canyon NP	.941	26	Gulf Islands NS	1.000	48	Redwood NP	.367	*Large Historic-Preserving Units*		
3	Canyonlands NP	1.000	27	Mammoth Cave NP	.785	49	Saguaro NM	1.000	66	Antietam NB	1.000
4	Capital Reef NP	1.000	28	Apostle Islands NL	1.000	50	Sequoia NP	.951	67	Chaco Canyon NM	1.000
5	Dinosaur NM	.942	29	Isle Royal NP	1.000	51	Yosemite NP	1.000	68	Chickamauga and Chattanooga NMP	1.000
6	Glacier NP	1.000	30	Pictured Rocks NL	1.000	52	Crater Lake NP	1.000			
7	Grand Teton NP	.614	31	Sleeping Bear Dunes NL	1.000	53	Craters of the Moon NM	.818	69	Colonial NHP	1.000
8	Great Sand Dunes NM	.814	32	Voyageurs NP	1.000	54	Mt. McKinley NP	1.000	70	Fredericksburg and Spottsylvania County Battlefield NMP	.987
9	Mesa Verde NP	1.000	33	Bandelier NM	1.000	55	North Cascades NP	.946			
10	Rocky Mountain NP	.894	34	Big Bend NP	1.000	*Classification #5*					
11	Theodore Roosevelt NP	.314	35	Canyon de Chelly NM	1.000	*National Recreation Areas*			71	Gettysburg NMP	1.000
12	Yellowstone NP	1.000	36	Carlsbad Caverns NP	1.000	56	Bighorn Canyon NRA	.372	72	Golden Spike NHS	1.000
13	Zion NP	.865	37	Guadalupe Mountains NP	1.000	57	Curecanti NRA	1.000	73	Horseshoe Bend NMP	.330
14	Arcadia NP	1.000	38	Wupatki NM	1.000	58	Glen Canyon NRA	1.000	74	Kennesaw Mountain NBP	1.000
15	Cape Cod NS	1.000	39	Death Valley NP	1.000	59	Delaware Water Gap NRA	1.000			
16	Prince William Forest NP	1.000	40	Grand Canyon NP	1.000	60	Cuyahoga Valley NRA	1.000	75	Kings Mountain NMP	.550
17	Assateague Island NS	1.000	41	Hawaii Volcanoes NP	1.000				76	Manassas NBP	1.000
18	Shenandoah NP	.779	42	Joshua Tree NM	1.000	61	Lake Merideth NRA	1.000	77	Nez Perce NMP	.706
19	Biscayne NP	1.000	43	Lassen Volcanic NP	1.000	62	Golden Gate NRA	1.000	78	Saratoga NMP	.535
20	Canaveral NS	.680	44	Lava Beds NM	.471	63	Lake Mead NRA	1.000	79	Shiloh NMP	.785
21	Cape Hatteras NS	1.000			.266				80	Valley Forge NHP	1.000
22	Cumberland Island NS	.481									

Figure 1. Distribution of Inefficient Values in Run 1
($N = 26$)

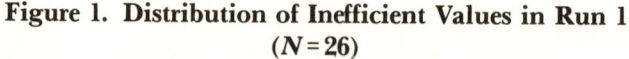

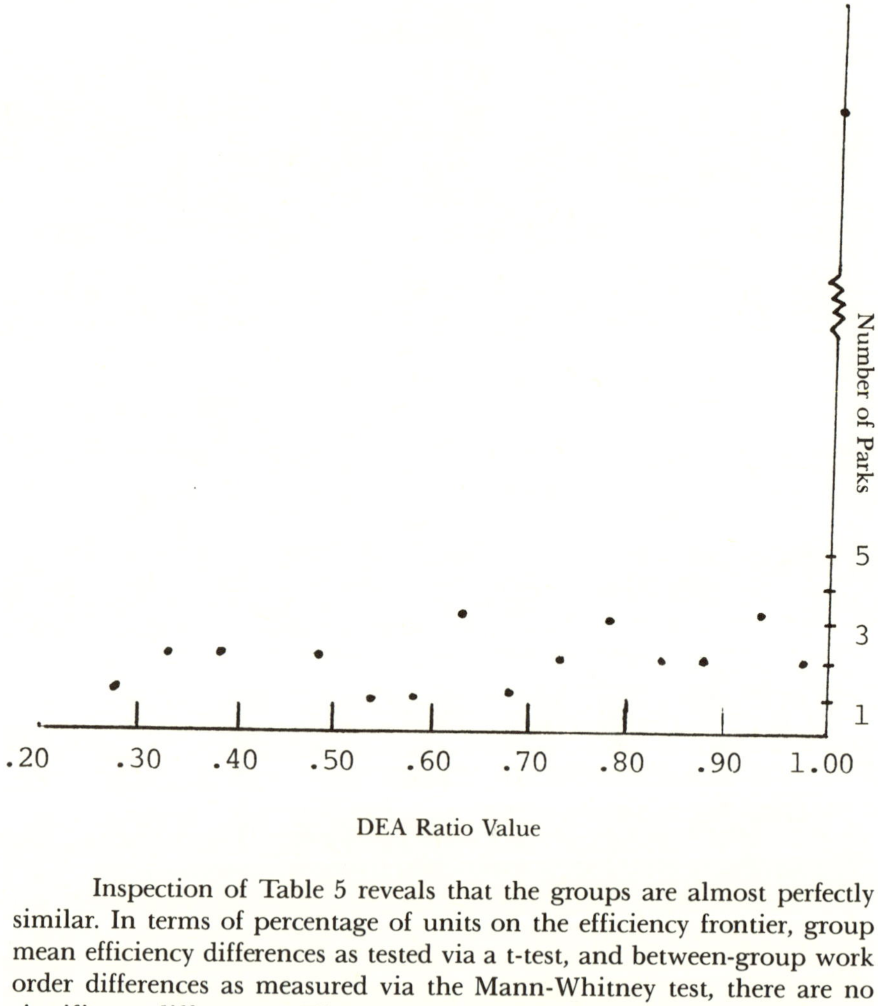

DEA Ratio Value

Inspection of Table 5 reveals that the groups are almost perfectly similar. In terms of percentage of units on the efficiency frontier, group mean efficiency differences as tested via a t-test, and between-group work order differences as measured via the Mann-Whitney test, there are no significant differences. There appear to be no systematic differences between land-preserving units and National Recreation Areas on the one hand and historic-preserving units on the other. The same is true for the parametric and nonparametric comparisons of national parks with other land-preserving units and National Recreation Areas and comparisons of National Recreation Areas with all land-preserving units, including national parks.

Naturally, we must not draw too firm a set of conclusions from the information just presented. Nevertheless, the three comparisons do strongly suggest the following: First, neither land-preserving units nor

Table 5. Park Group Comparisons

Type	#	Efficiency Mean	%$h_0 = 1$	t^a	p	Independent Samples
Land-Preserving	65	.8966	$\frac{44}{65}=.677$	0.6424		Z = .5362
Historic-Preserving	15	.8596	$\frac{9}{15}=.600$		p > .05	p > .05
National Parks	34	.9096	$\frac{23}{34}=.676$	0.5582		Z = .16417
Other Land-Preserving Serving & Recreational	31	.8823	$\frac{21}{31}=.677$		p > .05	p > .05
National Recreation Area	10	.8730	$\frac{7}{10}=.70$	0.4981		Z = .0272
Other Land-Preserving	55	.9008	$\frac{37}{55}=.673$		p > .05	p > .05

^{a} t-statistic = $\dfrac{\bar{x}_1 - \bar{x}_2}{\dfrac{n_1 s_1^2 + n_2 s_2^2}{n_1 + n_2 - 2} \dfrac{n_1 + n_2}{n_1 n_2}}$

historic-preserving units have a performance advantage over the other. Whether these two groups are defined as numbers likely to locate on the efficiency frontier, as mean efficiency ratio values, or as rank order of ratio values, they perform about the same. Arguments often heard in the agency that historic parks are shortchanged may be true. But, even if they are, the land-preserving units use the resources that they receive in a manner no worse than the historic-preserving units that may on the average receive fewer resources.

By the same token, the comparison between units that have been designated as national parks and other land-preserving units showed no differences in performance efficiency. Thus, while national parks may be favored with special resource support, they also have used these resources as well as other parks. In fact, while it is not significantly greater, the national parks actually have a higher mean performance efficiency than other land-preserving units and National Recreation Areas in the sample.

Finally, the comparison between National Recreation Areas and land-preserving units helps to put to rest the allegation that National Recreation Areas tend to underemphasize other park mission goals. Of course, it is possible for visitation or other recreation goals to receive more priority than other goals, but at least commitment to these other responsibilities has remained high enough that the group performance of the recreation areas does not drop.

However, these comparisons do not address our other policy questions relating to visitation and manpower levels. To gain some understanding of these questions, we must take some additional steps. To begin with, we must compute the ratio of the NVIS AREA/VIS AREA inputs. These ratio values provide an indication of the degree of park manpower usage relative to mission responsibilities in the visitation area. Of course, it is possible for a park to have a very high preservation responsibility, which can result in a high NVIS/VIS ratio due to the need to devote large areas of the park to preservation manpower and equipment or administrative needs. Also, if a park that receives extraordinary manpower resources emphasizes visitation, there could be a simultaneous increase in both NVIS and VIS AREAS. Nevertheless, some dimensions of the relation between manpower usage and responsibility are captured in this ratio value.

After computing these NVIS/VIS AREA ratio values, we compared the calculated DEA efficiency measurements for extreme groups in terms of this manpower indicator. One group consisted of the twenty parks that had the highest NVIS/VIS AREA ratio, while the other group was made up of the twenty units with the lowest NVIS/VIS AREA values. If there is extraordinary manpower usage in some parks, it is more likely to appear in parks with structural conditions that favor intense manpower levels, that is, in large nonvisitation areas relative to any other park working areas. Thus, high NVIS/VIS ratios may be accompanied by lower efficiency performance values.

In addition, as a more direct measure of a park's attention to visitation, we calculated the ratio between the total measured park planned contact with visitors defined in terms of the ratio of output variables TALK VIS plus TRIP VIS and the total number of visitor hours spent in the park (VIS HRS). The question is, Do the parks with high (TALK + TRIP VIS)/VIS HRS ratio values emphasize visitation more than the others? Again, we compare extreme groups, that is, the twenty parks with the highest (TALK VIS + TRIP VIS)/VIS HRS values with the twenty parks with the lowest ratio values. Consistent with the preceding arguments, parks with low ratios should be more likely to have efficiency values on the frontier. Table 6 displays these results.

The direction of the differences for both comparisons was consistent with the suspected relationships. The parks with the highest NVIS/VIS AREA ratios had more members on the efficiency frontier and were likely

Table 6. Manpower and Visitation Comparisons

Type	#	$\bar{h}_0$ Mean	Ratio $\frac{\#h_0 = 1}{Total}$	t^* (p)	Mann-Whitney Test Z (p)
Highest NVIS AREA/VIS AREA	20	.8651	$\frac{13}{20}$ = .65	1.175	1.0684
Lowest NVIS AREA/VIS AREA	20	.9394	$\frac{17}{20}$ = .85	(p > .05)	(p > .05)
Highest $\frac{\text{TALK VIS + TRIP VIS}}{\text{VIS HRS}}$	20	.84958	$\frac{12}{20}$ = .75	.46903	.6492
Lowest $\frac{\text{TALK VIS + TRIP VIS}}{\text{VIS HRS}}$	20	.88405	$\frac{13}{20}$ = .60	(p > .05)	(p > .05)

to have lower efficiency values than other parks. However, in no way can we conclude that overuse of manpower is rampant and that such overuse results in reduced performance. The difference between the two groups evaluated in terms either of the more powerful parametric t-test or of the Mann-Whitney rank order test were not statistically significant at our acceptance level of .05. For the visitation contact radio, the same conditions hold. While the highest contact group did make a poor showing, it was not significantly different from the lowest contact ratio group. It is evident from these comparisons that there are differences based on manpower or visitation levels. However, we must perform additional measurement and analysis before we can make more conclusive statements.

Conclusion and Summary

Given the weakness in existing measuring instruments, it was not my intention in conducting the study described in this chapter to arrive at a series of definitive policy or park management conclusions. Rather, my aim was to demonstrate an approach that can be used to answer certain types of natural resource management questions.

Proceeding first by applying DEA, then by comparing or examining the substance of several policy questions or management beliefs, it was possible to obtain some answers. My study suggests that there are fewer differences among classifications of parks than previously believed. Also, there may be misallocation of manpower resources. While high manpower usage is not concentrated in certain classifications of parks, it is more likely to result in decreased park performance.

While DEA can offer assistance in analyzing park operational behavior, three very serious problems or issues remain to be resolved. First, it is possible that time and dollar constraints prevented me from measuring significant process factors. Measurements on environmental conditions fall into this category. Second, there are major qualitative differences in units of services provided across parks that the model's surrogate variables do not capture. For example, the true output of trail use is not just the number of persons who use the trail but rather the aggregate quality of their trail experience. Third, more concrete measures of degrees of preservation are essential. Answers to the question of what is the output of the preservation process are still at a very primitive stage of development.

To some degree, the solution of these issues lies beyond the scope of current measurement tools. But, as such tools become available, the approach outlined here can easily accommodate these improvements, and the management evaluation that it provides will be strengthened as a result.

References

Banker, R. "Studies in Cost Allocation and Efficiency Evaluation." Unpublished thesis. Graduate School of Business Administration, Harvard University, 1980.

Banker, R. "Estimating Most-Productive Scale Size Using Data Envelopment Analysis." *European Journal of Operational Research,* in press.

Banker, R., Charnes, A., and Cooper, W. W. "Models for Estimating Technical and Scale Efficiencies in Data Envelopment Analysis." *Management Science,* 1984, *30,* 1078-1092.

Charnes, A., Cooper, W. W., and Rhodes, E. "Measuring the Efficiency of Decision-Making Units." *European Journal of Operations Research,* 1978, *2* (6), 429-444.

Charnes, A., Cooper, W. W., and Rhodes, E. "Evaluating Program and Managerial Efficiency: An Application of Data Envelopment Analysis to Program Follow Through." *Management Science,* 1981, *27* (6), 668-687.

Cicchetti, C. J., Fisher, A. C., and Smith, K. V. "Economic Models and Planning Outdoor Recreation." *Operations Research,* 1973, *2.*

Cultural Resource Division, National Park Service. *Cultural Resources Management and Guidelines.* Washington, D.C.: Cultural Resource Division, National Park Service, 1980.

Fisher, A., and Krutilla, J. V. "Determination of Optimal Capacity of Resource-Based Recreational Facilities." *Natural Resource Journal,* 1972, *12,* 417-444.

General Accounting Office. *Facilities in Many National Parks and Forests Do Not Meet Health and Safety Standards.* Washington, D.C.: General Accounting Office, 1980.

Lee, R. G. *The Management of Human Components in the Yosemite National Park Ecosystem.* San Francisco: National Park Service, 1975.

Liddle, M. J. "A Theoretical Relationship Between the Primary Productivity of Vegetation and Its Ability to Tolerate Trampling." *Biological Conservation,* 1975, *8,* 251-255.

National Park Service. *Management Guidelines.* Washington, D.C.: National Park Service, 1979a.

National Park Service. *Index of National Park System and Related Areas.* Washington, D.C.: National Park Service, 1979b.

National Park Service. *State of the Parks 1980: Report to the Congress.* Washington, D.C.: National Park Service, 1981.

Penz, A. A. "Outdoor Recreation Areas: Capacity and the Formulation of Use Policy." *Management Science,* 1975, 22, 139-147.

Rhodes, E. "Data Envelopment Analysis and Related Approaches for Measuring the Efficiency of Decision-Making Units with an Application to Program Follow Through in U.S. Education." Unpublished doctoral thesis. School of Urban and Public Affairs, Carnegie-Mellon University, 1978.

Schmidly, D. J., and Ditton, R. B. "Assessing Human Impact in Two National Park Areas of Western Texas." In *Proceedings of United States Forest Service Conference on Recreational Impact on Wildlands.* Washington, D.C.: U.S. Government Printing Office, 1978.

Shelby, B. "Crowding Models for Backcountry Recreation." *Land Economics,* 1980, 56, 43-55.

Smith, K. V., and Krutilla, J. V. "A Simulation Model for the Management of Low-Density Recreational Areas." *Journal of Environmental Economics and Management,* 1974, 1, 187-201.

Stankey, G. H. "A Strategy for the Definition and Management of Wilderness Quality." In J. V. Krutilla (ed.), *Natural Environments: Studies in Theoretical and Applied Analysis.* Baltimore, Md.: Resources for the Future, 1972.

Stankey, G. H. *Visitor Perception of Wilderness Recreation Carrying Capacity.* U.S. Department of Agriculture Forest Service Research Paper INT-142. Ogden, Utah: Intermountain Forest and Ranger Experiment Station, 1973.

Wildland Research Center, University of California. *Wilderness and Recreation: A Report on Resources, Values, and Problems.* Outdoor Recreation Resources Review Commission Study Report No. 3. Wildland Research Center, University of California, 1962.

Wise, J. A., and Cole, W. "The Use of Interpretive Structural Modeling in the Context of Recreational Impact Management." In *Proceedings of United States Forest Service Conference on Recreational Impact on Wildlands.* Washington, D.C.: U.S. Government Printing Office, 1978.

Eduardo L. Rhodes is associate professor in the School of Public and Environmental Affairs, Indiana University, Bloomington.

This chapter points out serious shortcomings in DEA's treatment of price efficiency, illustrates the dangers of misspecification errors in DEA, and suggests extentions of the basic DEA formulation that address these shortcomings.

Data Envelopment Analysis: Critique and Extensions

Thomas R. Sexton, Richard H. Silkman, Andrew J. Hogan

Chapter One presented and discussed the basic methodology of DEA. It was shown how the problem was formulated, how it was transformed into a linear program and solved, and how the solutions both to the DEA problem and to its dual can be interpreted. Managerial strategies that could be generated by DEA were described, and the process was illustrated with an example. Chapters Two and Three presented some detailed applications of DEA. These examples illustrate the power and utility of the methodology for assessing performance and for evaluating management and management strategies. In this chapter, we will describe some recent methodological advances that enable the analyst to extract additional information from the DEA methodology. These advances include the use of goal programming to develop cross-efficiencies, cluster analysis, analysis of variance, and pooled cross section time-series analysis. Before we do so, however, we will describe some of the shortcomings of data envelopment analysis.

Shortcomings of Data Envelopment Analysis

Price Versus Technical Efficiency. Consider again the nursing home example presented in Chapter One, where it was found that four of the six DMUs were perfectly efficient. This means that only DMUs E and F were logical targets for managerial improvements; DMUs A through D were as efficient as they could be, relatively speaking. And yet, DMUs A through D were very different one from another both in terms of the outputs that each produced and in terms of the technologies (input combinations) that each used to produce these outputs. An interesting question to ask is whether there are differences of both degree and kind among efficient DMUs and whether anything can be learned from close examination.

This is an important question to ask, since it is not uncommon for a sizable proportion of the DMUs to be efficient in DEA. Remember that we are solving linear programs with $n+1$ constraints (one for each DMU plus one equality constraint) in $(m+s)$-dimensional space (one dimension for each input and output). Whenever $m+s$ is large relative to n, we can expect many of the DMUs to find their optimal solution somewhere along the boundary of their own constraint, there being few other constraints to render this infeasible, because it is precisely along this boundary where a DMU is perfectly efficient. For this reason, it is advisable to limit the number of inputs and outputs used in DEA, selecting candidate variables only when we can be reasonably certain that they play a meaningful role in the operation of the DMUs.

Perfectly efficient DMUs are perfectly efficient in one important sense: They are technically efficient. This means either that, given its choice of technology, a perfectly efficient DMU cannot produce any additional output from its existing input mix or, alternatively, that any reduction in inputs will result in a reduction in output. There is no waste or slack. Data envelopment analysis is directed exclusively at the examination of technical inefficiency. DEA cannot be used to analyze or comment on a DMU's price efficiency. That is, DEA cannot say whether the DMU is producing the socially optimum (most highly valued) output mix using the least-cost technologies. The distinction between price and technical efficiency is nicely drawn and discussed by Farrell (1957), and it is important to understand, since a private firm or government agency—in fact, any DMU—can be technically efficient but price inefficient. Further, certain price-inefficient DMUs can actually produce their outputs at lower costs than certain technically efficient DMUs. While it is clearly important for organizations to operate in a productively efficient manner by maximizing the outputs from given inputs, it is often of more immediate concern for the typical public or not-for-profit sector organization that it produce socially beneficial outputs using ever shrinking and increasingly constrained financial resources. That is, price efficiency can be more important than technical efficiency. Should our schools emphasize "back to basics" instruction, our hospitals acute or chronic care delivery, our child welfare agencies foster care or adoption, our prisons punishment or rehabilitation? What is it that we desire from our organizations, and how does this affect our assessment of efficiency? Similarly, should park department inventories be computerized, nurse practitioners perform triage duties, security guards be accorded police powers, utility companies convert from oil to coal fired electricity generation? What are the least expensive ways of producing a desired output, and how do they affect our assessment of efficiency? These are questions of price efficiency, which is often very different from technical efficiency.

An illustration borrowed from Forsund and others (1980) may help to illuminate the key distinctions. Consider a firm that uses two variable inputs, X and Y, to produce a single output, Q, subject to constant returns to scale. Let $Q=1$ in Figure 1 represent a unit isoquant. If PP' represents a line of constant total costs for the two inputs, then C alone is perfectly efficient in the sense that there is no other way of producing $Q=1$ at lower costs. Note, however that B is technically efficient, since, given X and Y in proportion along ray OA, B specifies the minimum amounts of the two inputs required to produce $Q=1$. Nevertheless, B is not price efficient, because it costs more to produce $Q=1$ at B than it does at C, given input prices. The ratio OD/OB measures price efficiency. In contrast, A is both price and technically inefficient. By a similar argument, OD/OA and OB/OA measure price and technical efficiency, respectively, at A.

Obviously, it is possible both to be technically inefficient and to produce at lower costs than a similar organization that is technically efficient. In Figure 1, both F and G are technically efficient in the same sense in which B is. However, given the input prices of PP', neither point is price efficient. Indeed, while all the points lying within the area formed by $FBCG$ are technically inefficient, they are nevertheless less costly than either F or G. Waste or slack resources represent only one manifestation of the efficiency problem and not necessarily the most important. Use of input combinations that are outdated (for example, manual management information systems) or too costly (for example, failure to utilize paraprofessionals fully) can lead to large losses in efficiency.

Alternatively, we can view the output side of a multiproduct public or not-for-profit organization, for example, an elementary school. Consider the simple case of only two outputs, reading achievement and math achievement, denoted by R and M in Figure 2. ST represents the production possibilities curve for the school in that it indicates all possible combinations of reading and math achievements that can be produced with the inputs available. If VV' represents a line of constant total value, then C alone is perfectly efficient, since at C the social value of the school's output is maximized. As in Figure 1, other points besides C are technically efficient—B, for example. However, the social value of the output of the school at B is less than it is at C, since D, which lies on VV' and which hence has the same social value as C, lies beyond B. The ratio OB/OD serves as a measure of price efficiency. Similarly, at A, which is both price and technically inefficient, OA/OD indicates price efficiency, while OA/OB measures technical efficiency. The social value of an organization

Figure 1. A Simple Illustration of Price and Technical Efficiencies: Optimal Input Combinations

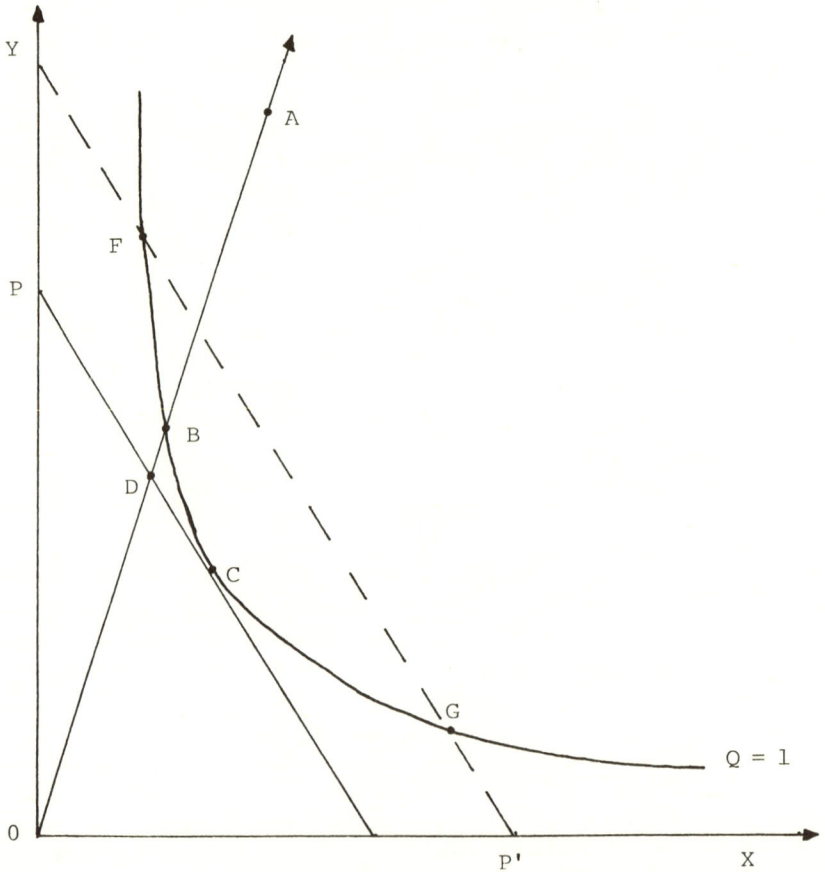

depends both on its ability to use resources efficiently, that is, to obtain the possibilities curve, and on its ability to produce outputs that society values. The elementary school that produces reading achievement at the expense of math achievement (point *B* in Figure 2) is likely in a society that values both about equally to be viewed as inefficient relative to other schools. In fact, productively inefficient schools in the region *BCG* will be viewed as more valuable than the technically efficient school at *B*. This element of inefficiency is missed when the focus is exclusively on production relationships.

Of course, the difficulty for attempts to incorporate price efficiency lies in the determination of relative societal values for an organization's outputs and/or resource opportunity costs for its inputs—in a word, the aggregation weights in the DEA linear programming specification (see

Figure 2. A Simple Illustration of Price and Technical Efficiencies: Optimal Output Combinations

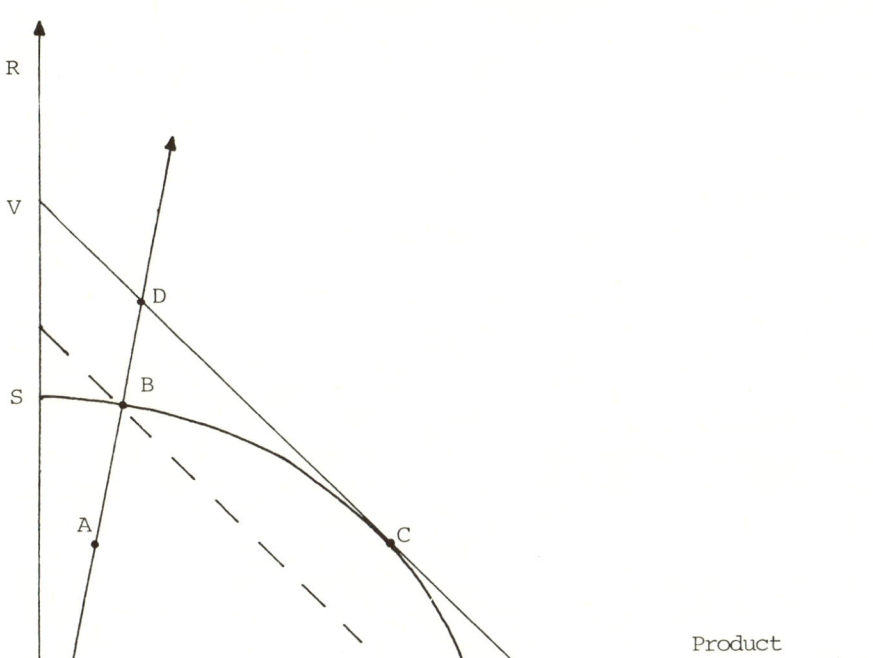

Chapter One). The usual approach is to use market prices when they are available and to impute them when they are not. The result is often far from satisfactory, because key variables are omitted from consideration due to the absence of acceptable prices or values. The DEA technique approaches the problem of aggregation weights from the opposite perspective in that it uses neither actual nor imputed market prices but rather allows each organization or DMU to select those weights subject to certain constraints. Further, the weights can be and generally are substantially different for each DMU. The result is that such points as S and T in Figure 2 are viewed as being equally efficient as C. Indeed, as we will argue later, since DEA employs extremal techniques, DMUs that use extreme input combinations or that produce extreme output mixes will be efficient by definition. Should we call an organization efficient because it is successful in maximizing its use, relative to comparable organizations, of the most expensive input while selecting an artificially low aggregation weight? Or, is a DMU efficient that engages in socially expensive specialization but that compensates by unilaterally declaring its output and only its output of any value? Clearly, there is a problem, and the problem lies with the exclusive focus on technical efficiency.

There is another more subtle but just as disturbing manifestation of this problem: the treatment of differential quality and the impact on technical efficiency. Imagine, for example, a well-functioning input market such that input price differentials perfectly reflect differences in productivity related to the quality of inputs. Imagine also two DMUs, each employing different quality levels of the input to produce similar outputs. Now, assume that each DMU is overall efficient; that is, the economic value of the outputs divided by the economic value of the inputs is maximized and equal for the two DMUs. When we view economic value, the differential quality problem is accounted for through pricing mechanisms in the input market. However, if we focus on physical output-input ratios and ignore quality differentials among inputs, then clearly the efficiency standard is determined by the agency that uses the most productive or highest-quality inputs. This remains true in the DEA framework, where there is an inclination to undervalue quality inputs for the purposes of computing efficiency. And, what is true on the input side is equally true but reversed on the output side, where the DMU that produces the higher-quality output is penalized. Without common and meaningful aggregation weights, it is imperative for outputs and inputs to be homogeneous.

Misspecification. All estimation techniques are subject to errors or biases introduced as a result of a wide variety of model misspecification problems. However, some techniques are more sensitive to certain problems than others are. For example, median-based estimation procedures are less sensitive to coding or data entry errors than mean-based procedures are. Similarly, ordinary or generalized least-squares techniques tend to be more robust over a wider range of model specifications than more sophisticated techniques that employ such procedures as instrumental variables. Generally speaking, however, estimation procedures, such as DEA, that rely on extremal points or observations are most sensitive to all types of specification problems, including variable selection, model specification, and coding or data entry errors. As Charnes and others (1978) emphasize, DEA is essentially a free-form technique not subject to prior specification of particular and rigid functional relationships. And yet, DEA can be very sensitive to model specification and errors in data. In the next two sections, we illustrate the kinds of problems that can arise when DEA is used in the presence of various types of specification error.

Errors in Data. In the previous section, we noted that, since data envelopment analysis is an extremal method, all extreme points are by definition efficient. Let us clarify this point somewhat. Since we are considering here an application involving inputs and outputs of production processes, we will define an extreme DMU as one in which the ratio Y_{rk}/X_{ik} is maximized over all k for any specific r,i combination; that is, the kth DMU represents the efficiency standard for that output-input pair. That this DMU must be efficient, consider choosing $u_r = 1$ and $v_i = 1$ for the specific r,i pair and all other u's and v's equal to zero. A simple calculation using the DEA formulation in Chapter One shows that these u and v vectors are feasible and that they yield an efficiency score of one for the extreme DMU.

This correspondence between extremity and optimality is disturbing for two reasons—first, because it will often lack statistical validity, second, because it is highly sensitive to errors in data. Both points are easy to illustrate.

Consider Figure 3, which plots the normalized outputs of a number of comparable DMUs. In this simple case, each DMU uses two variable inputs, L and K, to produce a single output. The lower envelop or efficient production isoquant is illustrated as it would be defined and calculated by DEA techniques. Note that each extreme technology (the maximum and minimum K/L) lies on the isoquant and that it is thus efficient. Now imagine dividing this quadrant into cones formed by rays from the origin at, let us say, successive fifteen-degree intervals. Each DMU in the sample and each point on the efficient isoquant will lie within one of the cones so formed. An interesting question to ask is whether there is any statistical difference between a segment of the isoquant that lies within a cone containing few observations (extreme technologies) and a segment that lies within a cone containing many observations (common technologies). Alternatively, we can ask how certain, in a statistical sense, one can be of those segments of an efficient isoquant constructed with very limited information. Clearly, in its traditional sense, statistical confidence depends on sample size: We feel more comfortable with those segments of the isoquant constructed from many comparable observations than we do with the segments constructed from only a few. The question then becomes, Do we more accurately describe efficient technologies in these extreme cones by relying on the few observations within them or by using the many observations in the central cones to predict out of sample? The trade-off is that the former preserves the nonparametric specification of production relationships, while the latter requires the production relationships to be functionally specified. We would argue that the answer is unclear.

The concern raised by errors in data is much less subtle and potentially far more serious than the statistical validity issue. What we mean to include here are such problems as misreported or miscoded data that plague research, especially where it involves evaluation of public sector programs or agencies. Since DEA is an extremal method, it is particularly

Figure 3. Facets of the Efficiency Frontier: Efficient Relative to What?

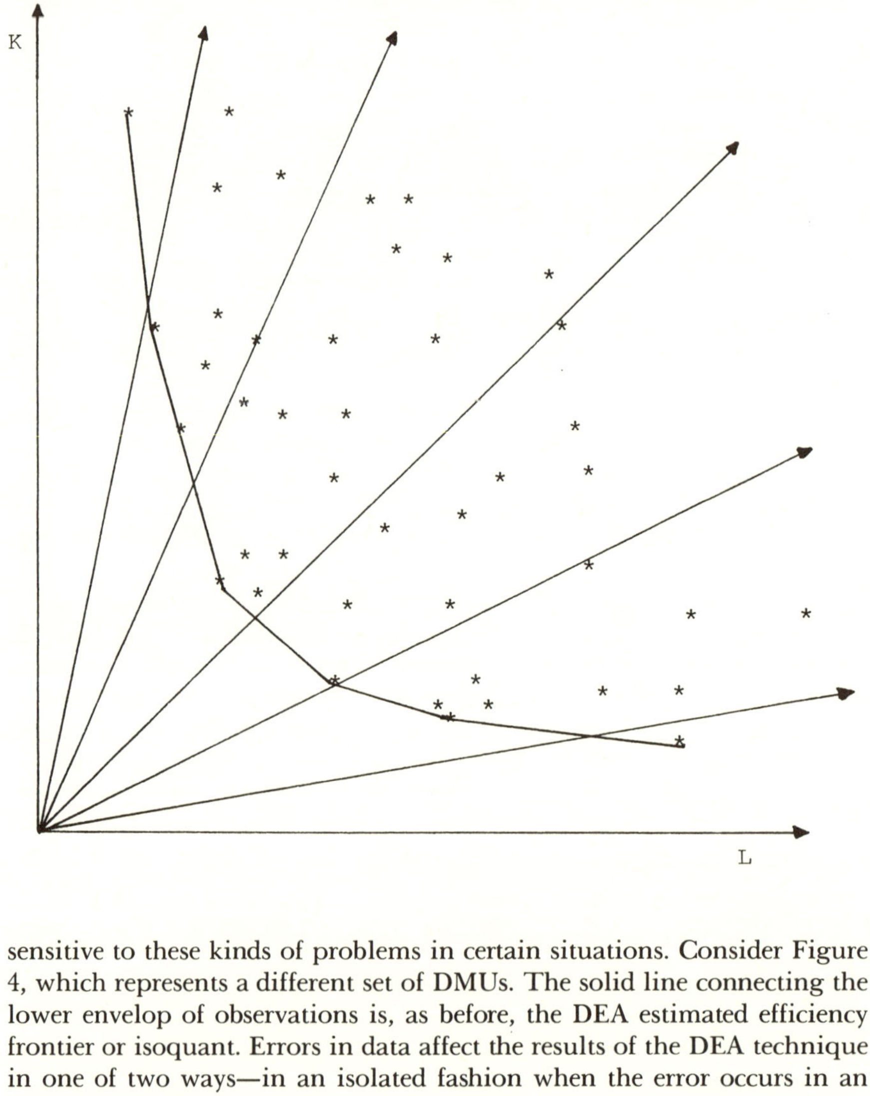

sensitive to these kinds of problems in certain situations. Consider Figure 4, which represents a different set of DMUs. The solid line connecting the lower envelop of observations is, as before, the DEA estimated efficiency frontier or isoquant. Errors in data affect the results of the DEA technique in one of two ways—in an isolated fashion when the error occurs in an observation off the frontier or in an interactive fashion when the error occurs in data pertaining to an efficient DMU. (Interactive errors can also occur when an inefficient observation is made efficient, as in the situation described later in this section.) In contrast, for regression techniques, all errors affect the estimated regression line and hence each and every observation. Interactive errors in DEA are the most troubling, since they alter the shape of the isoquant, which can affect many of the efficiency scores to one degree or another. To illustrate, assume that the correct observation

Figure 4. An Illustration of Two Types of Computational Errors Resulting from Errors in Data

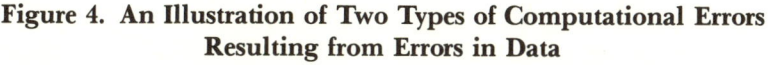

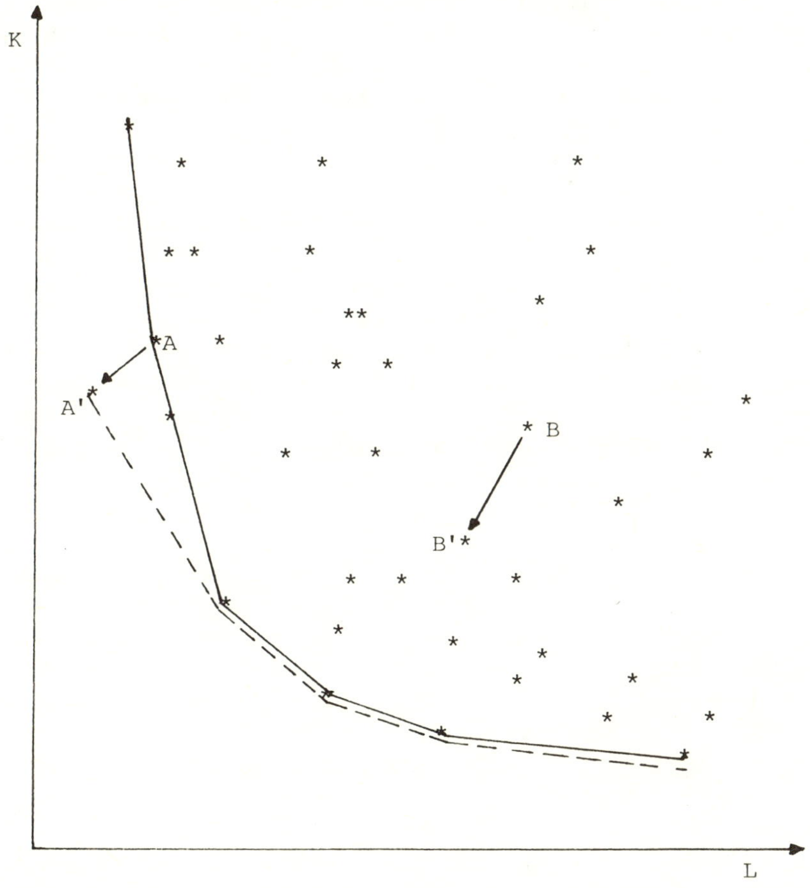

A was either misreported or miscoded as A' in Figure 4. The resulting isoquant (the dashed line) may be substantially different from the true isoquant, and it will cause many DMUs to be misclassified as less efficient than they actually are. In contrast, if an inefficient DMU is misreported as B' rather than B, the resulting error will be local, confined to that and only that DMU.

To us, there seems to be a trade-off between mean and extremal methodologies with regard to the effects of errors in data, one that is perhaps best understood in the context of the mean-variance analysis paradigm. On average, data errors will have broader though smaller quantitative impacts when mean-based methodologies are used. However, when serious errors occur, their impacts are magnified by extremal techniques, such as DEA.

Just how severe these errors can be is illustrated by Table 1, where we present the efficiency scores resulting from two DEA analyses based on the Program Follow Through (PFT) sites reported by Charnes and others (1981). The first run uses the data reported by those authors, while the second run changes only the level of the third output in the twenty-eighth DMU from 18.30 to 75.30. (In fact, this change actually occurred as a result of a simple data entry error.) As the most cursory comparison of the two runs makes clear, the results are very different. Average efficiency drops in the second run by 12 percent, with losers outnumbering gainers thirty-seven to one. Of the DMUs that were efficient after the first run, seven were no longer efficient after the second run. It is difficult to imagine the circumstances under which such an error could have such a large impact when a mean-based estimation technique was used.

We counsel users of data envelopment analysis to be well aware of its heightened sensitivity to errors in data and to use preprocessing error detection routines whenever and wherever possible. Because DEA fully utilizes the information contained in extreme values, the techniques traditionally used for recognizing outliers, such as residual plots, cannot be applied.

Variable Selection. Another major shortcoming of DEA lies in its failure to generate any measures either of statistical association or of causal relationships between the inputs and the outputs of the observed DMUs. Application of the DEA technique provides no information regarding the structural definition of the problem. Further, there is no way of assessing the relative strengths of different model specifications, since the calculated efficiency frontier perfectly explains the full set of extremal relationships under any specification. What criteria, then, do we use to choose among alternative model specifications, to include or reject inputs or outputs from the analysis?

This is a critical question, since we have already shown that any DMU using a maximum output-input ratio for any district that produces the highest reading scores per teacher employed is efficient; but, so is the school district that produces the highest reading scores per seat in its football stadium. The inclusion of irrelevant factors or even of noise in a DEA application will produce results that cannot be distinguished from the results of theoretically correct model specifications. A corollary to this is that virtually any DMU can be made to look efficient through the judicious though plausible and most likely quite defensible selection of outputs and inputs to be included.

This is by no means a trivial concern. For example, in their comparison of managerial and program efficiency, Charnes and others (1981) included three outputs and five inputs in their DEA specification, chosen from among a set of eleven outputs and twenty-five inputs. While they were careful to note that their application of DEA to Program Follow

Table 1. Sensitivity of Efficiency Scores to Data Entry Errors or Other Errors in Data

	Efficiency Scores		
Site	Data	Data with Error	Percent Change in Efficiency
1	1.000	1.000	0.0
2	.901	.729	-19.2
3	.988	.961	-2.4
4	.902	.642	-28.9
5	1.000	1.000	0.0
6	.907	.787	-13.3
7	.892	.657	-26.4
8	.914	.704	-23.1
9	.871	.664	-23.8
10	1.000	.959	-4.1
11	.982	.912	-7.2
12	.974	.974	0.0
13	.860	.649	-24.6
14	.984	.954	-3.1
15	1.000	1.000	0.0
16	.950	.754	-20.7
17	1.000	1.000	0.0
18	1.000	1.000	0.0
19	.950	.799	-15.9
20	1.000	1.000	0.0
21	1.000	1.000	0.0
22	1.000	.944	-5.6
23	.963	.785	-18.5
24	1.000	1.000	0.0
25	.976	.819	-16.1
26	.937	.737	-21.4
27	1.000	1.000	0.0
28	.944	1.000	5.6
29	.842	.685	-18.7
30	.902	.642	-29.0
31	.839	.587	-30.1
32	.907	.682	-24.9
33	.940	.778	-17.3
34	.852	.686	-19.5
35	.999	.753	-24.7
36	.803	.547	-31.9
37	.861	.706	-18.1
38	.948	.936	-1.0
39	.935	.751	-19.7
40	1.000	.934	-6.7
41	.946	.715	-24.5
42	.947	.903	-4.7
43	.870	.679	-22.1
44	1.000	1.000	0.0
45	.892	.808	-9.5
46	.908	.663	-27.1
47	1.000	.877	-12.4
48	1.000	.995	-0.6
49	1.000	.856	-14.5
Average Efficiency Score	.944	.828	

Through was only illustrative, one wonders under what conditions any application of DEA is not. How consistent are their conclusions for various combinations of this larger set of inputs and outputs?

We have looked at this question in a very limited way by using the data provided by Charnes and others (1981). In particular, we have tested three hypothetical cases: the consequences of including one additional input (the size of the program as measured by the number of students), the consequences of including one additional random input (a uniformly distributed variable over the interval 1 to 99 inclusive), and the consequences of selecting from among six variables (the five used by Charnes and others plus program size) only those that can be shown to be statistically significant determinants of at least one program output. We present the efficiency score for the base model and the three hypothetical cases in Table 2 for the PFT sites. Before we discuss the results, we need to clarify the third hypothetical case.

To test for the strength and magnitude of the relationships between each of the six inputs and each of the three outputs, we relied on the traditional procedure of estimating Cobb-Douglas type production functions separately for each of the outputs. While there are conceptual problems with this procedure—for example, the estimation of average and nonextremal production relationships and the disaggregation of an essentially joint production process—we feel that it is nevertheless useful and insightful. We note in passing that Bessent and others (1982) use an alternative statistical criterion, which relies on the simple correlation coefficient between, in their case, a single output and an array of feasible inputs. The results of these regressions that we performed are reported in Table 3. In response to these results, we elected to include all inputs statistically significant at the .05 level in at least one output case for the purposes of the third hypothetical.

The information in Table 3 raises a number of interesting questions. For example, how confident can one be in basing policy decisions involving such things as the reallocation of program resources on production relationships that explain less than half the variance in observed outputs? And, how do we know after having performed a DEA analysis what its explanatory power is? What impact does the inclusion of a statistically insignificant determinant of output have on the results of a DEA analysis? What is the effect if that variable is negatively related to output, as appears to be the case with Number of Teachers? Finally, does the significant negative coefficient on program size (Student Population) in one of the three cases suggest the presence of scale diseconomies? That is, does the assumption of constant returns to scale in the DEA methodology bias the efficiency score results in favor of smaller programs? We do not have answers to these questions. We raise them only to illustrate some of our concerns regarding the application of data envelopment analysis.

Table 2. Efficiency Scores Under Alternative Model Specifications: PFT Sites

		Model Specification		
Site	Base Case #1	With Number of Students #2	With Uniform Random Input #3	With Statistically Significant Variables #4
1	1.000	1.000	1.000	.990
2	.901	.902	.902	.898
3	.988	.988	.988	.988
4	.902	.902	.907	.902
5	1.000	1.000	1.000	1.000
6	.908	.934	.908	.924
7	.892	.911	.916	.911
8	.914	.915	.914	.894
9	.871	.871	.903	.852
10	1.000	1.000	1.000	1.000
11	.982	.982	1.000	.968
12	.974	.994	1.000	.989
13	.860	.865	.867	.865
14	.984	.984	.984	.959
15	1.000	1.000	1.000	.996
16	.950	.950	.950	.942
17	1.000	1.000	1.000	1.000
18	1.000	1.000	1.000	1.000
19	.950	.950	1.000	.950
20	1.000	1.000	1.000	1.000
21	1.000	1.000	1.000	1.000
22	1.000	1.000	1.000	1.000
23	.963	.963	.963	.963
24	1.000	1.000	1.000	1.000
25	.976	.976	1.000	.976
26	.937	.937	.938	.937
27	1.000	1.000	1.000	1.000
28	.944	.944	.944	.919
29	.842	.884	.844	.881
30	.902	.902	.902	.878
31	.839	.839	.864	.839
32	.907	.907	.907	.886
33	.940	.940	.966	.940
34	.852	.852	.855	.852
35	.999	1.000	1.000	1.000
36	.803	.850	.803	.850
37	.861	.924	.861	.914
38	.948	.950	.948	.927
39	.935	.935	.935	.920
40	1.000	1.000	1.000	.980
41	.946	.947	.947	.943
42	.947	.947	.967	.928
43	.870	.871	.873	.847
44	1.000	1.000	1.000	1.000
45	.892	.907	.891	.879
46	.908	.915	.908	.915
47	1.000	1.000	1.000	1.000
48	1.000	1.000	1.000	.971
49	1.000	1.000	1.000	1.000

Table 3. Coefficient Estimates from a Cobb-Douglas Production Function Specification

	Output Measure		
Input	Reading	Math	Cooper-Smith
Education of Mother	.108 (.063)	.020 (.062)	-.016 (.015)
Occupation Index	1.542** (.458)	1.431** (.454)	.412** (.111)
Parental Visit Index	-.581 (.422)	-.566 (.417)	-.093 (.102)
Counseling Index	-.658 (.358)	-.453 (.354)	-.206* (.087)
Number of Teachers	-.107 (.056)	-.131* (.055)	-.007 (.013)
Student Population	-.098* (.045)	-.087 (.045)	-.009 (.011)
Constant	1.512	1.437	-.412
R^2	.465	.342	.331
F-statistic	9.130**	5.458**	5.201**
N	70	70	70

Note: Figures in parentheses are the estimated standard errors of the coefficients.
 *indicates statistical significance at the .05 level.
 **indicates statistical significance at the .01 level.

The results displayed in Table 2 should come as no surprise. However, they serve to illustrate two principles that are worthy of discussion. The first principle is that efficiency scores cannot go down when additional variables, either inputs or outputs, are added to the model. As we have seen, each DMU performs at least as well under specification 2 as it does under specification 4. Similarly, each DMU performs as well under specification 2 as it does under 1 and as well under 3 as it does under 1. The regression analog is that the addition of one independent variable cannot reduce the overall predictive power of the model. It can, however, reduce its significance as measured, for example, either by the adjusted R-squared or by the F-statistic. Unfortunately, DEA produces no such interpretive information.

The second principle is that, at the margin, variable selection can be either critical or inconsequential, depending on how changes in model specification affect the shape and position of the efficiency frontier in the neighborhood of specific DMUs. For example, the efficiency score for site 3 is .988 for all four model specifications. A close look at the computed weights or virtual multipliers for this site reveals that all the input weight is placed on the counseling index and on number of teachers, neither of which is altered by any of the hypotheticals. Further, site 3 is of average size (Student Population = 58); coincidentally it was assigned an average random variable value of 49. Site 3 can be contrasted in this respect with site 40, which placed 99 percent of its computed input weight on Parental Visit Index. When this variable is eliminated from the analysis in specification 4, the site's efficiency score drops considerably. Attaching significant weight to an output or input is a necessary condition for changes in that output or input to produce changes in efficiency scores. That it is not also sufficient to produce such changes is illustrated by sites 62 and 67. The former placed 32 percent of its computed input weight on Parental Visit Index, yet it remains efficient even when the variable is omitted. The latter placed all its computed input weight on this input, and it is only marginally affected by its omission.

In light of these results, we argue that it is prudent procedure when using DEA to pay serious attention to the issue of variable selection. While the inclusion or omission of particular outputs or inputs will often prove either to be inconsequential or to have only limited, localized impacts, it can also have devastating consequences.

Extensions to Improve the Application of Data Envelopment Analysis

Data envelopment analysis is a very powerful data analysis technique that is especially useful in studying the productive behavior of public or not-for-profit organizations. However, as we note in the preceding section, the technique is not without its shortcomings, many of which can have very serious consequences for the computation and subsequent interpretation of results. In this section, we present a variety of procedures designed to reduce the hazard associated with data envelopment analysis. As with any powerful statistical technique, the best advice remains the judicious and prudent use of the technique. Our contribution here is to lay out a few simple procedures that will alert the DEA user to potentially serious problems in the analysis or interpretation of results.

Constraining Input and Output Weights. The key to incorporating price efficiency into the basic DEA analysis lies in focusing on the values of the input and output weights (virtual multipliers) contained in the complete solution to the linear programming problem. As Figures 1 and 2 show, price efficiency requires pairwise input and output price ratios to be equal to pairwise ratios of the input and output weights in the solution to the linear programming problem for each DMU. This is not to say that these weight ratios must be equal across DMUs; it says only that each DMU must respond to the price ratios that it faces. Thus, determination of price efficiency, requires knowledge of both the input and output prices faced by each DMU, knowledge that Charnes and others (1978) correctly argue is generally not available in many situations in which DEA is likely to be used. The result is an impasse: We are led to use DEA when we have limited or no knowledge of input or output prices, but such prices are essential if we are to compute price efficiencies.

One computationally simple technique that helps us to address this dilemma involves the imposition of constraints on the ranges over which some or all input or output weights are allowed to vary. Obviously, these restrictions should bear close resemblance on the output side to the goals and objectives of society and the organization and on the input side to the opportunity costs of acquiring additional resources.

For example, in the Program Follow Through case, it seems reasonable to argue that improvement in any of the three output measures—reading, math, or Cooper-Smith scores—is equally desirable; that is, their output weights should be equal. Imposing such a constraint in the DEA analysis forces each DMU to assess its operations in light of social or program objectives. As Table 4 shows, efficiency scores drop considerably on average when this constraint is imposed, reflecting the extent of output weight variation among PFT sites. Indeed, if we refer back to Figure 2, we can identify situations in which the aggregated output of technically efficient sites is actually less valuable given this weighting constraint than the outputs of technically inefficient sites. For example, site 35's efficiency score falls from 1.000 to .798, which is lower than the resulting scores of eleven of the thirty-two originally inefficient sites. In terms of Figure 2, if we view site 35 as a point, such as *B*, fully one-third of the originally inefficient sites fall within the area *BGC*. This simple diagnostic procedure suggests that, in this larger and arguably more important context, such sites as 35 and 16 are less efficient than one is led to believe, while such sites as 12 and 38 are relatively much more efficient than the initial DEA analysis would suggest.

Cross-Efficiency. Another way of addressing the issue of price efficiency is to subject each DMU to a range of input and output weights—not any range, but rather the range of weights chosen by the other DMUs in the analysis. This approach has the effect of computing what we have called a *cross-efficiency*, that is, the efficiency score that a particular DMU receives when it is rated by another DMU. A DMU can rate itself very highly, that is, it can have a very high efficiency score, but it can also be rated quite low by the majority of other DMUs. Such a DMU would be technically efficient while using a production technology unlike that of most other DMUs. While it is not possible to say with certainty that this DMU is price inefficient, the fact that it uses an input mix so different

Table 4. Efficiency Scores Constraining Output Weights to Be Equal: PFT Sites

Site	Unconstrained Efficiency Score	Constrained Efficiency Score	Percentage Decrease
1	1.000	.966	3.4
2	.901	.747	17.1
3	.988	.927	6.2
4	.902	.690	23.5
5	1.000	.945	5.5
6	.907	.816	10.0
7	.892	.661	25.9
8	.914	.701	23.3
9	.871	.684	21.5
10	1.000	.935	6.5
11	.982	.864	12.0
12	.974	.961	1.3
13	.860	.684	20.5
14	.984	.913	7.2
15	1.000	1.000	0.0
16	.950	.768	19.2
17	1.000	1.000	0.0
18	1.000	1.000	0.0
19	.950	.790	16.8
20	1.000	1.000	0.0
21	1.000	1.000	0.0
22	1.000	.966	3.4
23	.963	.808	16.1
24	1.000	1.000	0.0
25	.976	.801	17.9
26	.937	.776	17.2
27	1.000	.989	1.1
28	.944	.822	12.9
29	.842	.680	19.2
30	.902	.690	23.5
31	.839	.633	24.6
32	.907	.723	20.3
33	.940	.775	17.6
34	.852	.714	16.2
35	1.000	.798	20.2
36	.803	.571	28.9
37	.861	.714	17.1
38	.948	.926	2.3
39	.935	.771	17.5
40	1.000	.921	7.9
41	.946	.931	1.6
42	.947	.857	9.5
43	.870	.697	19.9
44	1.000	1.000	0.0
45	.892	.824	7.6
46	.908	.701	22.8
47	1.000	.935	6.5
48	1.000	.975	2.5
49	1.000	.890	11.0
Average Efficiency Score	.944	.817	13.5

from the majority of the other DMUs warrants some attention. An analysis of the cross-efficiency scores of each DMU calls attention to this and to other types of interesting DMUs.

We have defined the cross-efficiency of DMU j as measured by DMU k as the ratio of weighted output to weighted input obtained when we use the input and output levels of DMU j and the input and output weights derived for DMU k. Mathematically, the cross-efficiency is the ratio of the sums on the left side of constraint j in the (DEA) problem for DMU k:

$$E_{kj} = \frac{\sum_{r=1}^{s} u_{rk} Y_{rj}}{\sum_{i=1}^{m} v_{ik} X_{ij}}$$

The cross-efficiencies are simply the ratios in the constraints of the original fractional linear programming problem that we transformed into (DEA).

These cross-efficiencies are easily presented in an n-by-n matrix, where E_{kj} is the entry in row k, column j. We call this the *cross-efficiency matrix*. Observe that the usual efficiency values, now called *self-rated efficiencies*, lie along the diagonal of the cross-efficiency matrix.

By reading across row K of the cross-efficiency matrix, we can see how DMU k rates each of the other DMUs, that is, how efficient each of the other DMUs is when the optimal weights generated by DMU k are used to evaluate it. The mean efficiency in row k (including the diagonal) is called EROW (k); it measures the average efficiency of all DMUs according to DMU k.

In exactly analogous fashion, we can read down column j of the cross-efficiency matrix to see how DMU j is rated by each of the other DMUs when it is evaluated by means of the optimal weights that they generated. The mean efficiency in column j (including the diagonal) is called ECOL (j); it measures the average efficiency of DMU j according to all other DMUs.

Finally, we can compute the average of all the cross-efficiency values, called EBAR. This average will tend to be large when the DMUs select weights that are similar, thereby producing large cross-efficiencies; it can be used as a measure of concordance of production processes among the DMUs. Trivially, EBAR also equals the average value of the EROW (k) or, equivalently, the average value of the ECOL (j).

Before we illustrate these concepts in our example, we must first make a crucial observation: Whenever a DMU is perfectly efficient, its linear program (DEA) almost surely has multiple optimal solutions. To see this, consider the constraint corresponding to DMU k in its own version of (DEA):

$$\sum_{r=1}^{s} u_{rk} Y_{rk} - \sum_{i=1}^{m} v_{ik} X_{ik} \leq 0$$

Substituting the equality constraint from the same linear program yields

$$\sum_{r=1}^{s} u_{rk} Y_{rk} \leq 1$$

Notice that the left side of this inequality, which must be satisfied, is precisely the objective function of (DEA) for DMU k. Thus, (DEA) for DMU k contains an implicit constraint that is parallel to the objective function and that is binding when DMU k is perfectly efficient. Therefore, barring degeneracy at optimality, an efficient DMU will have multiple optimal solutions, that is, multiple sets of weights from which to choose.

This implies that the weights produced by (DEA) for efficient DMUs are somewhat arbitrary; they reflect simply the first optimal solution found by the simplex method. Consequently, the cross-efficiencies computed when these weights are used, as well as the EROW (k), ECOL (j), and EBAR derived from the cross-efficiencies, are also arbitrary and can thus be quite misleading.

One potential remedy is to use goal-programming techniques to impose a secondary objective function, which enters the analysis only for the purpose of tiebreaking at optimality. Let us see how goal programming operates in the general linear programming context.

Goal Programming. Suppose we are faced with a managerial situation in which several competing desiderata are potential objective functions. For example, a firm may wish simultaneously to maximize profit, minimize the need for expansion investment, and stabilize employment. We refer to these potential objectives as *goals*. The usual linear programming procedure is to select one goal to be the objective function and to relegate the rest to the constraint set, where we impose a minimum, maximum, or target level on each. The goal-programming procedure places all the goals into the constraint set and imposes a new objective function equal to a weighted sum of the deviations (in both directions but not necessarily equally weighted) of each goal from its minimum, maximum, or target level. Thus, the solution that is obtained will not maximize profit, minimize the need for expansion investment, or keep employment constant; rather, it will achieve a compromise among these goals based on the weights attached to the deviations.

In this example, the firm would select a minimum profit level (Pmin), a maximum capital investment level (Cmax), and a target employment level (Enow). Let d_P^+, d_P^-, d_C^+, d_C^-, d_E^+, and d_E^- represent the deviations above (+) or below (−) the corresponding levels (P = profit, C = capital investment, and E = employment). Clearly, then, no more than one of the two deviation variables in each pair can be positive; we can be above the stated level, below the stated level, or at the stated level. Whenever one of the variables in a pair is positive at optimality, the goal-programming formulation will guarantee that the other variable in that pair equals zero.

Next, the firm would set unit penalty weights on the unwanted deviations. Here, it would select values for w_P^-, w_C^+, w_E^+, and w_E^- to represent the penalties associated with having profit fall one unit short of Pmin, with requiring one unit of capital investment over Cmax, with requiring the addition of one unit of employment above Enow, and with requiring the reduction of one unit of employment below Enow, respectively. These weights will all be positive. In addition, the firm could specify negative weights associated with desirable deviations (for example, profit over Pmin), but we do not do this in DEA, so we will not do it here.

The firm would then use either the ordinary simplex method or some specialized goal-programming algorithm to solve the following linear goal program:

$$\text{Min } Z = w_P^- d_P^- + w_C^+ d_C^+ + w_E^+ d_E^+ + w_E^- d_E^-$$

subject to

$$Px - d_P^+ + d_P^- = \text{Pmin}$$
$$Cx - d_C^+ + d_C^- = \text{Cmax}$$
$$Ex - d_E^+ + d_E^- = \text{Enow}$$
$$Ax \leq b$$
$$x \geq 0 \qquad \text{all } d\text{'s} \geq 0$$

where x is a column vector of decision variables, P is a row vector of profit coefficients, C is a row vector of capital investment coefficients, E is a row vector of employment coefficients, A is a matrix of constants, and b is a column vector of constants. The constraints $Ax \leq b$ represent the set of other constraints in the problem that are not explicitly considered as goals.

Goal programming can be used to choose from among multiple optimal solutions in ordinary linear programming in the following way: We establish the objective function of the ordinary linear program as our primary goal and then select some other linear function of the decision variables as a secondary goal. The secondary goal should represent a quantity that is to be optimized only in the event of multiple optimal solutions in the original linear program and that should be ignored if the linear program has a unique optimal solution.

We accomplish this distinction between the goals by prioritizing them. To do this, we select unit weights that differ by several orders of magnitude. We might use unit weights of one million for the primary goal and of one for the secondary goal (after, of course, adjusting for any difference in the units of measurement used for the two goals). Such a large difference in objective function coefficients ensures that the optimal solution will optimize only the first goal unless multiple optimal solutions exist, in which case the set of multiple optimal solutions can be used as the feasible region to optimize the secondary objective.

This idea can be extended to several goals. The firm in our example might choose maximization of profits as its primary goal, minimization of capital investment as its secondary goal, and stabilization of employment as its tertiary goal. It would then set w_P^- equal to, say, one trillion, w_C^+ equal to one million, and w_E^+ and w_E^- each equal to one. Other weights would work equally well. The goal program would seek to maximize profits. If it found multiple solutions that all yielded the same optimal profit, it would choose from among the ones that minimized capital investment. If there were multiple solutions that simultaneously maximized profit and minimized capital investment, it would search among them for the ones that also stabilized employment. There is seldom need for more than two or three goals to reach a unique solution. A complete discussion of linear goal programming can be found in Schniederjans (1984).

We can apply goal programming to DEA in the following manner: We choose the maximization of DMU k's own efficiency, that is, the usual objective function, as its primary objective. Refer now to the formulation called (DEA) in Chapter One. Let d_{kj}^- be the slack variable associated with the constraint corresponding to the DMU j. (The goal-programming technique would allow us to place additional deviational variables d_{kj}^- into these constraints as well, but we do not wish to permit any DMU to have a cross-efficiency greater than one, so these d_{kj}^+ must all vanish.) Using the last constraint, it is easy to establish that the self-rated efficiency of DMU k, h_k, is 1 - d_{kk}^-, the maximization of which is equivalent to the minimization of d_{kk}^-. Our primary goal, then, is to minimize d_{kk}^-.

There are a number of possible secondary objectives. We will introduce two that lead to what we refer to as the *aggressive* and the *benevolent* formulations. The aggressive formulation assumes that, given a choice among several alternative solutions that maximize a DMU's self-rated efficiency, the DMU will choose the one that makes the other DMUs as inefficient as possible. In other words, it will choose weights that maintain its own efficiency rating while diminishing its cross-efficiency ratings of the other DMUs as much as possible. The benevolent formulation attempts the opposite: It chooses weights that maintain the DMU's self-efficiency rating while enhancing its cross-efficiency ratings of the other DMUs as much as possible.

We can operationalize these ideas using the deviational variables d_{kj}^-. We can see that:

$$\bar{d}_{kj} = \sum_{i=1}^{m} v_{ik} X_{ij} - \sum_{r=1}^{s} u_{rk} Y_{rj}$$

is the difference between the weighted input of DMU j and its weighted output when the weights generated by DMU k are used. While this difference is not the cross-efficiency E_{kj}, which is a ratio, it nonetheless captures the same idea, and, because it is linear, it offers an attractive surrogate for true cross-efficiency.

Under the aggressive formulation, then, we would seek to maximize the sum of the $\bar{d}_{kj}$. Under the benevolent formulation, we would seek to minimize this sum. The appropriate objective function is

$$\text{Minimize } Z^{\pm} = \bar{w}_k \bar{d}_{kk} \pm \sum_{\substack{j=1 \\ (j \neq k)}}^{n} \bar{w}_j \bar{d}_{kj}$$

where we choose the minus (plus) sign for the aggressive (benevolent) formulation and where we set all the $\bar{w}_j$ equal to one another and several orders of magnitude less than $\bar{w}_k$. In fact, these problems can easily be written without recourse to the deviational variables as follows:

$$\text{(DEA } \pm \text{) Maximize } Z^{\pm} = \sum_{r=1}^{s} u_{rk} \left(Y_{rk} \pm \delta \sum_{\substack{j=1 \\ (j \neq k)}}^{n} Y_{rj} \right) \pm \sum_{i=1}^{m} v_{ik} \left(\delta \sum_{\substack{j=1 \\ (j \neq k)}}^{n} X_{ij} \right)$$

subject to

$$\sum_{r=1}^{s} u_{rk} Y_{rj} - \sum_{i=1}^{m} v_{ik} X_{ij} \leq 0 \qquad j = 1, \ldots, n$$

$$\sum_{i=1}^{m} v_{ik} X_{ik} = 1$$

$$u_{rk} \geq 0 \quad r = 1, \ldots, s$$
$$v_{ik} \geq 0 \quad i = 1, \ldots, m$$

where now we choose the upper (lower) sign for the aggressive (benevolent) formulation and where δ is set several orders of magnitude below one.

We are now prepared to examine the cross-efficiencies in the example from Chapter One involving the six nursing homes. Refer to Table 4 in Chapter One for the optimal weights and self-rated efficiencies under the original formulation (DEA). Four of the six DMUs are perfectly efficient, indicating that the optimal weights presented for DMUs A through D in that table are not unique. Table 5 and Table 6 show analogous results for the aggressive and benevolent formulations, respectively, where we set δ = 0.0001.

A few observations are in order. First, notice that the self-rated efficiencies are identical in all three formulations, as they should be. The secondary objectives come into play only when the DMU is perfectly efficient and never at the expense of self-rated efficiency. Second, the weights selected by inefficient DMUs E and F are also identical under all three formulations. This follows for exactly the same reason. Third, the weights for the efficient DMUs in the aggressive formulation clearly reflect their specialist natures. Recall that the ratio analysis displayed in Table 2 of Chapter One indicated that DMU A had the largest ratio of MCPD to

Table 5. The Optimal Weights and Efficiencies Using the Aggressive Formulation

	Input Weights		Output Weights		
DMU	StHr	Supp	MCPD	PPPD	Efficiency
A	0	5.000	0.714	0	1.000
B	0	1.429	0	0.476	1.000
C	0.313	0	0.238	0	1.000
D	0.192	0	0	0.238	1.000
E	0.110	0.513	0.115	0.304	0.977
F	0.155	0.722	0.162	0.427	0.867

Table 6. The Optimal Weights and Efficiencies Using the Benevolent Formulation

	Input Weights		Output Weights		
DMU	StHr	Supp	MCPD	PPPD	Efficiency
A	0.517	1.121	0.505	0.837	1.000
B	0.138	0.642	0.144	0.380	1.000
C	0.172	0.374	0.168	0.279	1.000
D	0.069	0.321	0.072	0.190	1.000
E	0.110	0.513	0.115	0.304	0.977
F	0.155	0.722	0.162	0.427	0.867

Supp. In Table 5 of this chapter, we see that DMU A places all its output weight on MCPD and all its input weight on Supp. Similar remarks hold for DMUs B through D. Conceptually, the aggressive formulation forces DMUs to distinguish themselves from their peers as much as possible whenever they can achieve their first-priority goal: perfect efficiency. Observe that the reserve is true under the benevolent formulation: There, the efficient DMUs distribute their weights across all inputs and outputs in an effort to raise the cross-efficiencies that they dispense.

Table 7 shows the cross-efficiency matrices under the aggressive formulation, and Table 8 shows them under the benevolent formulation. Both tables also present the values of EROW, ECOL, and EBAR. Note that the self-rated efficiency scores lie along the diagonal of each matrix. A striking observation in Table 7 is the generally low cross-efficiency values that the efficient DMUs grant to one another in the aggressive formulation. On reflection, this is not surprising. Each efficient DMU specializes in converting one kind of input into one kind of output and chooses its weights accordingly. When these weights are applied to a DMU that specializes in a different kind of conversion, the resulting cross-efficiency is likely to be low. Contrast this with the results obtained from the benevolent formulation, in which the four efficient DMUs evaluate one another quite highly, even perfectly in some cases. In this small example, the efficient DMUs seem to have considerable latitude in selecting their weights.

The EROW and ECOL values also deserve some attention. Under the aggressive formulation, the ECOL values range from 0.608 to 0.764—not a very large spread but certainly an improvement over the self-rated efficiencies, four of which equal one. If we interpret (ECOL) (j) as another measure of the efficiency of DMU j, since it does represent an average view, then we would conclude that DMU A was the most efficient and that DMU C was the least efficient of the four DMUs with perfect self-rated efficiency. In fact, DMU C appears worse than DMU E, which does not rate itself perfectly. This contrasts rather sharply with the multiple regression results given in Chapter One while it is in agreement with the general assessment of DMU C, which was based on the fact that DMU C did not show up in any efficient reference set. Not unexpectedly, the benevolent formulation produces ECOL values that are much higher. But, once again, DMU C comes out the poorest among the efficient DMUs and worse than DMU E.

The EROW values are harder to interpret. EROW (k) is simply the average cross-efficiency of all DMUs when measured with the weights produced by DMU k. We have found empirically—and it remains true in this small example—that EROW and ECOL tend to be negatively correlated. Thus, DMUs that receive generally high cross-efficiency scores tend to give generally small scores in return. We could speculate on the significance of this phenomenon, but we will settle for pointing it out.

Table 7. The Cross-Efficiencies with EROW, ECOL, and EBAR Using the Aggressive Formulation

DMU	A	B	C	D	E	F	EROW
A	1.000	0.286	0.500	0.200	0.226	0.286	0.416
B	0.583	1.000	0.292	0.700	0.694	0.714	0.664
C	0.711	0.267	1.000	0.410	0.414	0.333	0.522
D	0.289	0.650	0.406	1.000	0.884	0.580	0.635
E	1.000	1.000	0.830	1.000	0.977	0.867	0.946
F	1.000	1.000	0.830	1.000	0.977	0.867	0.946
ECOL	0.764	0.700	0.643	0.700	0.696	0.608	0.688
							EBAR

Table 8. The Cross-Efficiencies with EROW, ECOL, and EBAR Using the Benevolent Formulation

DMU	A	B	C	D	E	F	EROW
A	1.000	0.864	1.000	1.000	0.968	0.805	0.939
B	1.000	1.000	0.830	1.000	0.977	0.867	0.946
C	1.000	0.864	1.000	1.000	0.968	0.805	0.939
D	1.000	1.000	0.830	1.000	0.977	0.867	0.946
E	1.000	1.000	0.830	1.000	0.977	0.867	0.946
F	1.000	1.000	0.830	1.000	0.977	0.867	0.946
ECOL	1.000	0.955	0.886	1.000	0.974	0.847	0.944
							EBAR

As we expected, the value of EBAR under the aggressive formulation (0.688) is much lower than the value of EBAR under the benevolent formulation (0.944). The value of EBAR under the original formulation—a somewhat arbitrary number due to the multiplicity of solutions in four of the six cases—is intermediate (0.738). Recall that EBAR can be interpreted as a measure of concordance among the DMUs regarding the weights selected; the aggressive formulation leads to considerably less agreement than the benevolent formulation does.

Which formulation should the analyst use? The answer depends on the situation and on the information that is sought. If all that we require is the self-rated efficiency scores and the dual variables for constructing managerial strategies, then the original formulation will be sufficient. But, if the input and output weights themselves are of interest, say for the purpose of identifying specialists, then the aggressive formulation is superior. And, if the cross-efficiencies and their related measures EROW, ECOL, and EBAR are sought, then either the aggressive or the benevolent formulation could be used. Naturally, nothing prevents the analyst from using any other secondary goal to break ties as long as the goal is meaningful and as long as it results in a model that is amenable to solution.

Our preference in most cases is to apply both the aggressive and the benevolent formulations and to examine the change in ECOL (j) for each DMU. This difference captures the sensitivity of DMU j to the harshness of its peers, and it is useful for identifying DMUs that are operating far from the crowd. Such DMUs are often perfectly efficient, but they have low values of ECOL, because their optimal weights are so different from those of their peers. We call such DMUs *mavericks*.

Finally, we note that the dual problem is affected only slightly by the introduction of the aggressive or benevolent secondary goals and that the managerial strategies produced from the original formulation can easily be extracted from the goal-programming versions presented earlier. We will not present the details here.

Clustering. The optimal weights selected by a DMU, especially under the aggressive formulation, are indicators of the production process employed by the DMU. As we have seen, DMUs that specialize in the conversion of a particular input into a particular output will place positive weights on that input and output, perhaps at the exclusion of all others. In any case, the optimal weights reflect the evaluation scheme under which the DMU is as efficient as possible. It follows, then, that DMUs which select similar weighting patterns are likely to use similar production processes and that the weights themselves can be used to form clusters of similar DMUs.

In some applications, such clustering can provide the analyst with additional insight regarding the DMUs. For example, a large set of nursing homes under analysis is likely to contain DMUs with widely varying characteristics. The set might include proprietary as well as nonprofit homes with differing organizational structures that lead to differing operating styles. It might also include skilled nursing facilities and health-related facilities that serve distinct patient populations. If the DMUs within a certain subpopulation do indeed employ similar production processes, the optimal weights can be used to detect this, and the analyst will have learned something specific about the distinction among the subpopulations.

We must make one important observation concerning optimal weights before we attempt to use them in a clustering procedure: The weights are scale dependent. That is, DMUs that use lower levels of inputs and outputs—the smaller DMUs—will generally have larger weights than the larger DMUs. To understand why, consider again the formulation labeled (DEA) in Chapter One. The last constraint acts to normalize the input weights by forcing the sum of the products of the input weights and the input levels to equal one. Thus, smaller DMUs, which have lower input levels, will require higher input weights to satisfy this constraint. The output weights then adjust to the input weights in order to satisfy the DMU's own maximum efficiency constraint. Therefore, two DMUs operating with the same production process but on different scales will place positive weights on the same inputs and outputs, but they will select appropriately scaled values that differ substantially.

While there may be several ways of normalizing the weights that thereby make them comparable, we have selected the following procedure, because it is simple and because it appears to capture the essence of the production process. We define binary (row) vectors C_r of length $m + s$ as follows:

$$C_k = (\bar{v}_{1k}, \bar{v}_{2k}, \ldots, \bar{v}_{mk}, \bar{u}_{1k}, \bar{u}_{2k}, \ldots, \bar{u}_{sk}) \qquad k = 1, \ldots, n$$

$$\bar{v}_{ik} = 1 \quad \text{if} \quad v_{ik} > 0, \quad \bar{v}_{ik} = 0 \quad \text{if} \quad v_{ik} = 0, \quad \bar{u}_{rk} = 1$$

$$\text{if} \quad u_{rk} > 0, \quad \text{and} \quad \bar{u}_{rk} = 0 \quad \text{if} \quad u_{rk} = 0.$$

$$\bar{v}_{ik} \text{ and the } \bar{u}_{rk}$$

In other words, the $\bar{v}_{ik}$ and the $\bar{u}_{ik}$ are merely indicators that equal one wherever DMU k has placed positive weight and that equal zero elsewhere. We refer to C_k as the *characterization vector* of DMU k. If two DMUs employ similar production processes, we can expect that they will possess similar characterization vectors.

Geometric interpretation can help us to visualize these vectors. Imagine a unit cube in three dimensions, that is, a cube in which each edge has length one. Imagine further that the cube has one vertex at the origin and that the entire cube lies in the quadrant where all coordinates are positive. Then, the eight vertices of this cube will have coordinates (0,0,0), (0,0,1), (0,1,0), . . . , (1,1,1); that is, the vertices of the cube will be the set of all possible three-dimensional characterization vectors. If $m + s = 3$, we could then visualize each DMU resting at some vertex of this cube. DMUs resting on the same vertex have the same characterization vector and are said to be *similar of degree zero*.

Consider two DMUs resting on adjacent vertices, say (0,1,0) and (0,1,1). Adjacent vertices are identified by the fact that their coordinates fail to match in exactly one position, position three in this example. We say that these two DMUs are *similar of degree one*.

What about two DMUs resting on nonadjacent vertices, such as (1,0,1) and (0,1,1)? We can define the distance between these vertices as the number of positions in which they fail to match, two in this case. This is a perfectly well-defined distance function, known as the L^1 *metric,* , which can be interpreted as the length of a shortest path between the two vertices where the paths are restricted to follow along the edges of the cube. The usual straight-line distance in which paths may cut across a face of the cube or even through its interior is called the *Euclidean* or L^2 *metric*. We would then say that these two DMUs were *similar of degree two*.

We are now prepared to generalize to higher dimensions. The characterization vectors now correspond to the vertices of the $(m + s)$ - dimensional version of the unit cube, which is called the *unit hypercube*. And, the L^1 metric still works: The distance between two characterization vectors is defined as the number of coordinates in which they fail to match. If this distance equals D for some pair of DMUs. then we say that these DMUs are *similar of degree* D. We can interpret D as the number of inputs and outputs over which the DMUs disagree in their weighting patterns.

The characterization vectors for our example involving the six nursing homes under the aggressive formulation are given in Table 9, and the L^1 distances are presented in Table 10. We see that inefficient DMUs E and F are similar of degree zero but that all other pairs of DMUs are at least two units apart. Thus, there are five clusters, four containing one efficient DMU each and one containing the two inefficient DMUs. This finding corresponds perfectly with our earlier observation that the four efficient DMUs really did operate with different production processes; this procedure simply formalizes the method for systematically reaching such conclusions.

We point out here that, had we used the benevolent formulation, all six DMUs would have had the same characterization vector, namely (1,1,1,1,1,1). Thus, all six DMUs would have fallen into one cluster, and little insight would have been gained. This illustrates again the discriminatory capabilities of the aggressive formulation.

In applications involving more DMUs, we could use the distance matrix to enlarge the clusters, thereby creating fewer of them. This would be helpful to us in interpreting the results. For example, we might imagine merging clusters that were somehow close to one another. After grouping together DMUs that were similar of degree zero, we could calculate the distance between the clusters simply by using the distances between any two representative DMUs, one from each cluster. Clusters that were one unit apart could then be merged. We introduced the notion of cluster seeds to handle this problem; we refer the reader to Sexton and others (1985) for the details.

Table 9. The Characterization Vectors Using the Aggressive Formulation

	Inputs		Outputs	
DMU	StHr	Supp	MCPD	PPPD
A	0	1	1	0
B	0	1	0	1
C	1	0	1	0
D	1	0	0	1
E	1	1	1	1
F	1	1	1	1

Table 10. The Distance Matrix

	DMU					
DMU	A	B	C	D	E	F
A	0	2	2	4	2	2
B	2	0	4	2	2	2
C	2	4	0	2	2	2
D	4	2	2	0	2	2
E	2	2	2	2	0	0
F	2	2	2	2	0	0

Analysis of Covariance. Following a DEA, one might wish to investigate the dependence of the computed efficiency scores upon variables that are not explicitly contained in the inputs and outputs. In a nursing home application, for instance, one may be interested in both the directions and the magnitudes of the effects of ownership type (proprietary, nonprofit, public), size, setting (urban, suburban, rural), and other variables on efficiency. These are essentially facility characteristics that may indirectly affect the nature and relative mixes of a DMU's inputs and outputs and that may not have been included in the DEA formulation.

One approach to this problem is to use analysis of covariance, in which the DEA efficiency score of the DMU is the dependent variable and the omitted variables are incorporated as either factors (categorical variables) or covariates (continuous variables). Analysis of covariance can be viewed as a generalized version of both multiple linear regression and analysis of variance, the first of which best handles continuous variables and the second of which is designed for categorical variables. A general analysis of covariance provides the statistical machinery necessary to estimate the coefficients and factor levels and then to test them for statistical significance. We will not describe the procedure here. The reader can consult virtually any text on multivariate statistics—for example, Seber (1977)—for details. However, it is appropriate to observe that self-rated efficiencies may have too little variation for an effective analysis and that ECOL values may thus be preferred. In either case, it is important to use an estimation procedure that explicitly constrains the dependent variable to be less than one.

One case in which this analysis of covariance procedure is especially useful is the case in which DEA is used in a dynamic or time-series context. The basic DEA model implicitly assumes that all observations relate to a single common time period. However, some efficiency evaluations require us to include multiple time periods. One example arises in analysis of the efficiency effects of a particular policy initiative or intervention. In a nursing home application, the analyst might be concerned with estimating the impacts on efficiency of a new reimbursement scheme for some patients. The analyst would collect input and output data over two periods, one before the change and one after, and attempt the appropriate comparisons. The analyst might also want to know the differential effects of the policy initiative or intervention on proprietary and on nonprofit homes. In another case, a regulatory agency might wish to conduct ongoing DEA as a routine monitoring device. Here, comparisons would be required over several time periods.

The standard approach is to pool all time periods and to perform one DEA in which each DMU is present T times, where T is the number of time periods. The efficient DMUs will then be some mixture of the DMUs from the different time periods. In the before or after situation just described, the effect of the policy initiative can be gauged by the prevalence of postinitiative or postintervention DMUs among the efficient DMUs and by the average efficiency gain (or loss) between the first and second periods. In the monitoring context, the average efficiency would be computed for each time period.

In this analysis of covariance extension, the DMU efficiency scores, either self-rated scores or cross-efficiencies, represent computer measures of productivity, a distillation of inputs and outputs into a single measure of performance. And, as with any such single measure, the variance in the indicator across observations can be due to chance, to the omission of relevant explanatory factors, or to real differences in technical efficiency. Distinguishing between the last two sources of variance is particularly difficult in public sector applications because of the difficulty inherent in developing meaningful measures of output quality on the one hand and in completely specifying the full range of goods and services provided on the other. Thus, we saw both Sherman in Chapter Two and Rhodes in Chapter Three taking great care to interpret the DEA findings in light of concerns regarding quality measurement and output specification. Sherman approached the problem by very narrowly defining the scope of interest and concern of his effort to the medical-surgical center of otherwise very similar teaching hospitals in Massachusetts. The covariation problem is reduced through sample stratification. In contrast, Rhodes looked at a much broader and more varied set of DMUs and addressed the same problem through the multiple specification of models. In this way, he was able to preserve a large sample size and thus to test relatively rich and complex input-output relationships. Of course, he runs a greater risk of comparing apples with oranges in the process.

In some respects, the analysis of covariance extension represents a compromise between these two extremes. However, it is not without its problems, the major one being that it permits the possibility of associating variation in efficiency scores to other variables, where such association is due to chance or to some spurious correlation. Further, once such association is identified and determined to be legitimate, it is not at all clear how the computer efficiency scores should be modified to incorporate this new information, since the efficiency scores and associations derive from two separate and unrelated mathematical computations. For example, if we find that size affects the computer efficiency scores of nursing homes, should we recompute size-adjusted scores (and if so, how), or have we identified a real issue for public policy concerning the industry structure and use this information as a component of overall management strategy? If we take the former option, a natural approach would be to incorporate the identified covariate as inputs in an expanded DEA model and to recompute the efficiency scores. However, this approach is less than satisfactory for categorical variables where no metric is meaningful, and it could dramatically alter the set of efficiency scores for all the DMUs in the analysis.

Clearly, this is an important problem with a number of possible, albeit less than perfect, solutions. Just as clearly, the existence of this problem in no way invalidates the DEA methodology, any more than the problem of multicollinearity invalidates multiple regression analysis. Rather, it means that considerable care must be exercised in the application of DEA and in subsequent interpretation of its results.

Conclusion

As data envelopment analysis becomes more widely used, its basic formulation has become much enhanced, making it at once more powerful and more useful. In this chapter, we have presented a number of ways in which the output from the basic DEA problem can be analyzed to provide decision makers with additional information. We do not suggest that these modifications and enhancements are inclusive or that they are even representative of what exists in the literature, where even the most cursory survey reveals modifications ranging from mathematically sophisticated extensions to such areas as production economies or diseconomies of scale to intuitive and straightforward application of the basic technique to such areas as Medicaid reimbursement for nursing home expenditures. Further, as this technique is diffused and as increasing numbers of researchers (especially in the social and behavioral sciences) use it to analyze the performance of decision-making units, we fully anticipate additional modifications, enhancements, and extensions, all of which will make DEA both more accessible and more useful.

References

Bessent, A., Bessent, W., Kennington, J., and Reagan, B. "An Application of Mathematical Programming to Assess Productivity in the Houston Independent School District." *Management Science*, 1982, *28* (12), 1355-1367.

Charnes, A., Cooper, W. W., and Rhodes, E. "Measuring the Efficiency of Decision-Making Units." *European Journal of Operational Research*, 1978, *2* (6), 429-444.

Charnes, A., Cooper, W. W., and Rhodes, E. "Evaluating Program and Managerial Efficiency: An Application of Data Envelopment Analysis to Program Follow Through." *Management Science*, 1981, *27* (6), 668-687.

Farrell, M. J. "The Measurement of Productivity Efficiency." *Journal of the Royal Statistical Society, Series A,* 1957, *120* (2), 253-290.

Forsund, F. R., Knox-Lovell, C. A., and Schmidt, P. "A Survey of Frontier Production Functions and of Their Relationship to Efficiency Measurement." *Journal of Econometrics*, 1980, *13*, 5-25.

Schniederjans, M. J. *Linear Goal Programming*. Princeton, N.J.: Petrocelli Books, 1984.

Seber, G.A.F. *Linear Regression Analysis*. New York: Wiley, 1977.

Sexton, T. R., Silkman, R. H., and Hogan, A. "Data Envelopment Analysis: Critique and Extensions." Working paper, Harriman College, State University of New York at Stony Brook, 1985.

Thomas R. Sexton is associate professor in the W. Averell Harriman College for Policy Analysis and Public Management, the State University of New York at Stony Brook.

Richard H. Silkman is associate professor of public policy and management in the Graduate Program in Public Policy and Management at the University of Southern Maine, Portland.

Andrew J. Hogan is associate professor in the Office of Medical Education, Research, and Development, in the College of Human Medicine, Michigan State University, East Lansing.

Index

A

Abraham Lincoln Birthplace National Historic Site, 48
Aggregation weights, 76–78
Aggressive formulations, 93, 96, 98, 100
Anthony, R. N., 36, 45
Atkinson, J. G., 45

B

Banker, R., 49, 70
Benevolent formulations, 93, 96, 98, 100
Bentley, J. D., 32, 38, 45
Bessent, A., 10, 28, 84, 104
Bessent, W., 28, 104
Best Linear Unbiased Estimator (BLUE), 5
Biles, B., 32, 45
Blue Ridge Parkway, 56–57
Bowlin, W. F., 32, 34, 46
Brookings Institution Economic Policy, 49
Butler, P. W., 32, 38, 45
Byrnes, P., 28

C

Capitol Building, 57
Characterizations vectors, 99
Charnes, A., 2, 6, 10, 29, 44, 46, 49, 70, 78, 82, 84, 104
Cicchetti, C. J., 48, 70
Cluster seeds, 100
Cobb-Douglas type production functions, 84
Cole, W., 48, 71
Computer efficiency scores, 103
Cook, T. J., 29
Cooper, W. W., 2, 6, 29, 46, 70, 104
Cooper-Smith scores, 88
Covariance analysis, 12, 101–103
Covariates (continuous variables), 102
Cross-efficiency matrix, 90

Cultural Resource Division, National Park Service, 52, 70

D

Data envelopment analysis (DEA): advantages of, 8, 44; clustering of DMUs in, 98–101; compared with other techniques, 43–44; computer systems for, 11; covariant analysis and, 101–103; cross-efficiency and, 12, 88–91; defined, 2, 25; of DMUs, 10–12; dual of, linear program, 23–26; effective use of, 3–4; example of, 19–23, 26–27; extremal nature of, 77, 79, 81; goal programming and, 91–98; graphical approach to, 2–17; of hospitals, 35–45; improvement of, 87–103; limitations of, 27–28, 44, 73–87; managerial value of, 11–12; Massachusetts hospital study using, 35–43; methodology of, 7–28; misspecification with, 78–87; of national parks, 50–69; noise in, 82; output-input relationship in, 2–3, 10, 36, 38, 74, 87–91; programming formulation of, 17–19; regression analysis and, 5; of relative efficiency, 10; of scale effects, 28; of technical efficiency, 74; uses for, 44–45
Decision-making units (DMUs): clustering of, 98–101; cross-efficiency of, 88–91; DEA of, 10–12; defined, 2; efficiency frontier and, 15; extreme, 79; input and output of, 12–13; maverick, 98; price-inefficient, 74; technically efficient, 74
Department of Interior, 47–48, 51
Diagnosis related groups (DRGs), 32, 38
Ditton, R. B., 48, 71
Dual of linear program, 23
Dual variables, 23–24

E

Econometric techniques, 33–35
Efficiency: data envelopment analysis

Efficiency *(continued)*
of, 10-12; DMU, 15; multiple regression analysis of, 9-10, 20-21; of national parks, 47-70; perfect, 74, 96; price, 74, 87-88; ratio, 15; ratio analysis of, 8-9, 33-34; social values and, 75-78; teaching hospital, 35-45; technical, 74

Efficiency frontier: changes in model and, 86-87; defined, 3; of DMUs, 13, 15, 80; in industry, 34; physical construction of, 15; redefinition of, 16

Efficiency reference set (ERS), 15, 23, 24, 26, 39-40

Efficient production isoquant, 79

Extremal techniques, 32, 77-78

F

F-statistic, 86
Factors (categorical variables), 101-102
Fare, R., 10, 28, 29
Farrell, M. J., 74, 104
Feldstein, M., 32, 33, 34, 35, 46
Fisher, A. C., 48, 70
Forsund, F. R., 10, 29, 32, 46
Forsund, M. J., 75, 104
Full-time equivalents (FTEs), 33, 36, 40, 42, 45
Functional Mathematical Programming System (FMPS), 11

G

Gateway National Recreation Area, 56
General Accounting Office, 32, 34, 46, 48, 70; study of U.S. hospitals, 33
Gettysburg National Military Park, 48
Glen Canyon National Recreation Area, 56
Goal programming, 91-98
Golden Gate National Recreation Area, 59
Grace, P., 6
Grace Commission report, 1-2
Grosskopf, S., 28

H

Harpers Ferry National Historical Park, 48
Health care: costs of, 31-32; efficiency measurement techniques for, 33-35; reimbursement mechanisms of, 32; standards of, 31. *See also* Hospitals
Hillier, F. S., 11, 29
Hogan, A., 104
Hospital Bureau, Massachusetts Rate Setting Commission, 33, 34, 46
Hospitals: DEA analysis of, 35, 43-44; management strategies of, 42-43; ratio analysis of, 33-41; regression analysis of, 34-35; study of Massachusetts teaching, 35-43; technical efficiency of, 44-45. *See also* Health care

I

Input/output weights, 2-3, 10, 36, 38, 49, 74, 87-91
International Mathematical Subroutine Library (IMSL), 11
Isoquant, 28, 75, 81

K

Kennington, J., 28, 104
Knox-Lovell, C. A., 29, 46, 104
Krutilla, J. V., 48, 70, 71

L

L^1 metric, 100
L^2 (or Euclidean) metric, 100
Lake Mead National Recreation Area, 56
Least squares techniques, 5, 20, 34, 78
Lee, R. G., 48, 70
Lewin, A. Y., 10, 29
Liddle, M. J., 48, 70
Lieberman, G. J., 11, 29
Linear fractional program, 11, 18
Linear programming: complementary slackness theory in, 24; dual in, 23-26; duality theory, 24; sensitivity analysis, 18; theory, 23

M

Management strategies: and DEA, 44; for DMUs, 12, 23; for hospitals, 42-43
Mann-Whitney test, 66, 69

Massachusetts Rate Setting Commission, 34, 46
Mean-based estimation procedures, 78, 82
Mean-variance analysis paradigm, 81
Median-based estimation procedures, 78
Medicaid, 32, 104
Medicare, 32
Misspecification errors: in data, 78-82; and variable selection, 82-87
Monitrend reports, 34
Morey, R. C., 29
Multiple regression analysis: drawbacks of, 9-10; example of, 20-21; model of organizations, 9. *See also* Regression analysis

N

National lakeshores, 64
National Mall, Washington, D.C., 56-57
National monuments, 64
National Park Service (NRS), 47-48, 50-53, 70, 71
National parks: DEA study of, 50-69; function surrogate variables of, 53-59; management challenges of, 48; management objectives of, 52, 54-58; mission of, 49-53; model of, 51; natural resource management of, 49-50; performance studies of, 48-49; protective and administrative functions of, 52
National Recreation Areas (NRAs), 57, 63-64, 66-67
National Register of Historic Places, 53
Nunamaker, T. R., 10, 29

O

Office of Policy Analysis, Department of Interior, 49, 51
Operations research, 2

P

Penz, A. A., 48, 71
Perfect efficiency, 74, 96
Preferred provider organizations (PPOs), 32
Price efficiency, 45, 75-77
Primont, D., 10, 29
Producing unit: efficiency frontier and, 3; inefficient, 3; objectives of, 2-3. *See also* Decision-making units
Program Follow Through (PFT), 82, 84, 88

R

R-squared, 86
Ratio analysis: appeal of, 34; of hospitals, 33-34; limitations of, 8-9, 33
Reagan, B., 28, 104
Redwood National Park, 63
Reese, J. S., 36, 45
Regression analysis: econometric techniques of, 33-35; of hospitals, 34; least squares method of, 5, 20, 34, 78; limitations of, 9-10, 34-35. *See also* Multiple regression analysis
Rhodes, E., 2, 6, 10, 29, 46, 49, 70, 71, 104

S

Schmidly, D. J., 48, 71
Schmidt, P., 29, 46, 104
Schniederjans, M. J., 93, 104
Schramm, C. J., 45
Seber, G.A.F., 102, 104
Secretary of Interior, 49
Self-rated efficiencies, 90
Sexton, T. R., 100, 104
Shelby, B., 48, 71
Sherman, H. D., 10, 29, 32, 34, 35, 36, 38, 40, 44, 46
Silkman, R. H., 104
Similar degree of . . . , 99-100
Simplex method, 11, 18, 24, 91
Smith, K. V., 70, 71
Software: for analysis of covariance, 12; for DEA, 11
Stankey, G. H., 48, 71

T

t-test, 66, 69

U

Unit hypercube, 100

V

Virtual multipliers, 87

W

Washington Monument, 57
Wildland Research Center, University of California, 71
Wise, J. A., 48, 71
Wolf Trap Park for the Performing Arts, 56

Y

Yellowstone National Park, 47
Yosemite National Park, 47

STATEMENT OF OWNERSHIP, MANAGEMENT AND CIRCULATION

U.S. Postal Service

1A. TITLE OF PUBLICATION	1B. PUBLICATION NO.	2. DATE OF FILING
New Directions for Program Evaluation	4 4 9 0 5 0	9/26/86

3. FREQUENCY OF ISSUE	3A. NO. OF ISSUES PUBLISHED ANNUALLY	3B. ANNUAL SUBSCRIPTION PRICE
Quarterly	4	$30 indv/$40 inst

4. COMPLETE MAILING ADDRESS OF KNOWN OFFICE OF PUBLICATION

433 California St., San Francisco (SF County), CA 94104

5. COMPLETE MAILING ADDRESS OF THE HEADQUARTERS OF GENERAL BUSINESS OFFICES OF THE PUBLISHER

433 California St., San Francisco (SF County), CA 94104

6. FULL NAMES AND COMPLETE MAILING ADDRESS OF PUBLISHER, EDITOR, AND MANAGING EDITOR

PUBLISHER (Name and Complete Mailing Address)

Jossey-Bass Inc., Publishers, 433 California St., S.F., CA 94104

EDITOR (Name and Complete Mailing Address)

Mark Lipsey, Psychology Dept., Claremont Graduate School, Claremont, CA 91711

MANAGING EDITOR (Name and Complete Mailing Address)

William Henry, Jossey-Bass Publishers, 433 California St., S.F., CA 94104

7. OWNER

FULL NAME	COMPLETE MAILING ADDRESS
Jossey-Bass Inc., Publishers	433 California St., S.F., CA 94104
For names and addresses of stockholders, see attached list.	

8. KNOWN BONDHOLDERS, MORTGAGEES, AND OTHER SECURITY HOLDERS OWNING OR HOLDING 1 PERCENT OR MORE OF TOTAL AMOUNT OF BONDS, MORTGAGES OR OTHER SECURITIES

FULL NAME	COMPLETE MAILING ADDRESS
Same as #7	

9. FOR COMPLETION BY NONPROFIT ORGANIZATIONS AUTHORIZED TO MAIL AT SPECIAL RATES

☐ (1) HAS NOT CHANGED DURING PRECEDING 12 MONTHS
☐ (2) HAS CHANGED DURING PRECEDING 12 MONTHS

10. EXTENT AND NATURE OF CIRCULATION	AVERAGE NO. COPIES EACH ISSUE DURING PRECEDING 12 MONTHS	ACTUAL NO. COPIES OF SINGLE ISSUE PUBLISHED NEAREST TO FILING DATE
A. TOTAL NO. COPIES (Net Press Run)	2200	2295
B. PAID AND/OR REQUESTED CIRCULATION		
1. Sales through dealers and carriers, street vendors and counter sales	1255	1415
2. Mail Subscription (Paid and/or requested)	476	424
C. TOTAL PAID AND/OR REQUESTED CIRCULATION	1731	1839
D. FREE DISTRIBUTION BY MAIL, CARRIER OR OTHER MEANS SAMPLES, COMPLIMENTARY, AND OTHER FREE COPIES	87	162
E. TOTAL DISTRIBUTION (Sum of C and D)	1768	2001
F. COPIES NOT DISTRIBUTED		
1. Office use, left over, unaccounted, spoiled after printing	432	294
2. Return from News Agents		
G. TOTAL (Sum of E, F1 and 2 - should equal net press run shown in A)	2200	2295

11. I certify that the statements made by me above are correct and complete

Vice President

PS Form 3526, Dec. 1985